Loves ♥
Holiday

Loves ♥ Holiday

MONICA LYNN

purposely
created
PUBLISHING

LOVES HOLIDAY

Published by Purposely Created Publishing Group™

Copyright © 2020 Monica Lynn

All rights reserved.

Printed in the United States of America

ISBN: 978-1-64484-302-4

Special discounts are available on bulk quantity purchases by book clubs, associations and special interest groups. For details email: sales@publishyourgift.com or call (888) 949-6228.

For information log on to www.PublishYourGift.com

Happy Holidays

To the reader, my love, I hope you enjoy this novel as much as I enjoyed writing it.

I hope you get everything you asked for this holiday season.

I hope your holiday is filled with love, joy, presents, God-filled blessings, and plenty of food. Save me a plate, I'm coming over.

Love and God bless,
Monica Lynn

DEDICATIONS

To my wonderful mother, thank you for the love and support, and for reminding me that my best days are ahead of me. To my brother Steven, sister-in law Ronda, and my beautiful niece Maegan for being there when I need you all the most. Sheridian Tiffany, CJ, Alicia, Savannah (S), and my best and close friend, Edward Brown, thank you all for believing in me. Uncle Tydie, thanks for the best advice growing up. I'll always remember you telling me to prove them wrong. Last but not least, to my beautiful aunts Lauren, Adrienne, Donna, Karen, Debbie, and Ruenay (Nay) whom I always looked up to for inspiration. I love you all.

Dedicated in loving memory to my grandmother, Eula Mae Webb. I love you forever. Michael Manieri, the best friend a girl could ever have. I miss you dearly. I wish you were here to share this moment with me. Uncle's Harold Mason and Keith Wayne Hayes, thanks for the laughs. Uncle Keith, I still look for you to come through that door screaming my name, "MONIBABY!" Russell Beverly, thank you for the good times. Last but not least, to Craig Desmond Lockes Sr. I always looked up to you as a father figure. Thank you for introducing me to class and sophistication. Thank you for coming into our lives and taking me to see Terry McMillian's *Waiting to Exhale*.

That was the moment I knew that this is what I wanted to do for the second half of my life. Thank you. May you all continue to shine your lights on us and rest in peace, until we meet again.

TABLE OF CONTENTS

Chapter One

·))))))) · (((((((·

INTRODUCTION
TO REALITY

Ashanti Bond-Harris

I am tired as hell. The customers will not stop coming in. It is a revolving door. *Lord, if one more person walks through this door.* As soon as I am done with one table, I got another table or I'm running food for servers that are way too busy with their other tables. I am about to pass out. Jaime Harris, executive chef, owner of Pete's, and my soon to be ex-husband, has me closing all this week, except for Thursday. Van Smith, his fraternity brother and childhood friend, is closing Thursday. The only reason why Van is closing Thursday is because he can't close Friday, so we switched. I would rather close Friday and open Saturday morning. That way, I can get all my Friday evening paperwork over and done with.

Jaime knew exactly what he was doing when he scheduled me on the late shifts. Ever since we parted ways, he has been an asshole and I don't like it. I left a bottle of Pellegrino water on his desk and he flipped out on me. Mama said he is going through something with the impending divorce. Well, Mama, he's the one that put us through this. I wanted to work on the marriage. I am tired. I tried. I will be cordial. I will go as far as acting like a civilized adult because of the business. Other than that, I really don't have anything to say to him.

And on top of all this madness, to add a cherry to my disaster sundae, a snowstorm is coming with up to a foot of snow expected. I'm not ready for that nonsense. You'd think people would be out getting toilet paper, eggs, and milk. Nope. They are here at Pete's, dining on nickel buffalo wings and ranch fries. The ranch fries here are life. I'm not even going to lie to you.

Van and Stephan are here with me tonight closing. Stephan is the assistant manager. Van is the general manager. Van also manages the Annapolis, Towson, and DC locations.

I thought having two of the best managers on shift with me would make tonight easier. I thought wrong. They were busy as well. Stephan got stuck online expediting. Van was running around the restaurant, keeping up with the weather, and helping out because so many people called out due to the impending storm. It does look creepy over the horizon; it definitely looks like it is about to snow.

I don't know what it is about an impending snowstorm, but I get all warm and fuzzy inside. It brings out the absolute worst in people, but I love it.

The one thing I can say about my staff is that they are not lazy. We have an awesome team here at the Inner Harbor location. Out of the five locations that we have, this location is the best. We have our ups and downs of course.

Jaime is home sick with the flu. I don't think anything is wrong with him though. He went out with some of the guys that work in the kitchen last night. I heard they had a great time. Jaime footed the bill. Whenever Jaime pays, everyone has a good time.

Stephan said that they got drunk and spent a lot of money at the strip club. Stephan didn't go. He's gay. He said he overheard some of the guys in the bar talking. My husband loves to spend money. Jaime's philosophy is work hard, play harder.

God, I can't believe that Jaime and I are having problems. I thought we were going to be married forever. Six months ago, I gave birth to a beautiful and healthy chocolate baby boy. The baby is with my mother. When I get off, I don't care what time it is, I am going to get my baby. I miss him. He may be sleep by the time I get to Mama's house, he might not. It depends on if Mama put him down for a nap or not, probably not. My baby, Jaime, never sleeps. I fall asleep before he does. He's the happiest little piece of chocolate. I want to kiss and hug him all day, but I have to work. Thinking about him makes me smile and gets me through the day. Going home to my baby makes this worth it.

I finally had a free chance to check in on the baby. I dipped into the hallway between the kitchen and the walk in, pulled my cell phone from my apron, and called

Mama. We're not supposed to have our cell phones on the floor, but who really listens? Jaime will be online expediting while talking on his cell phone. Plus, I want to keep my phone on me just in case he calls giving us the order to close.

I don't care if the staff have their cell phones as long as it does not interfere with work. Jaime can be a hard ass, but he's also soft as a marshmallow.

Jaime and I are currently separated. I'm trying to stay positive. I have to remain strong for my child and the business. We've been living apart for a year. I didn't want this. He did. He said there's no one else. I believe him. I am looking forward to the day that we are back together. He says he needs his space. I respect his decision. I don't want him to stay if he is unhappy. Jaime has been under a lot of stress. I fully understand. It's not easy running popular, lucrative businesses. It's enough to make you go crazy.

"Aunt Shanti."

That's my niece, Monica. She woke me out of my daze. I was just about to call Mama when she came to get me.

"You have a table."

Swazette, one of the seasoned hostesses, sat a party of two in my section. I gathered my tired thoughts, put on a smile, and went to greet my table.

"Thank you, Love," I smiled.

I really need to get it together.

Being in the restaurant industry is similar to being an actor. You have to put on a happy face even when you don't feel like it. You have to smile, giggle, and pay attention. I'm ready for my close up. I walk out on the floor and notice that it is getting darker and darker. I reach into my pocket and check my phone. Van walks up next to me. He is well put together and fine as hell. He smells so good.

"Jaime said he's paying close attention to the news."

I nodded as Van walked away towards the kitchen, scrolling through his iPhone. I have no idea what generation it is but it's a nice ass phone, better than mine, and I have the latest. I inhaled, exhaled slowly through my nose, then headed over to the table.

It doesn't take long for the couple to decide on the crab cake appetizers and baby back ribs for entrées, loaded baked potatoes, and green beans. Our green beans are delicious. Jaime uses my aunt Belle's recipe. They are greasy, down home, southern fried, fat back with the ham slice green beans. They are so good. The barbecue ribs are smoked to perfection and fall off the bone.

I put in the order then went into Jaime's office and closed the door. It's no bigger than a linen closet. It's always messy. He said it always looks messy because it is small. No, he's messy.

Jaime wants to buy more property here at the Harbor. He needs office space. He said he's going to lease some office space in The Gallery Mall for human resources. Jaime works from home.

♥

Pete's has been named the best soul food restaurant in Baltimore six years in a row. It is the best restaurant in Baltimore hands down. We've been featured on food television shows and we've won countless awards. I cannot count how many times local and cable news outlets have been to the restaurant for stories and features, especially around the holidays. We have a PR person specifically for that.

We are packed on the weekends. Don't bother coming during the football or baseball season. It is a mad house. When the Orioles or the Ravens play home games, you can forget about getting in on game night. If you are not here by a certain time, come back tomorrow. We are busy from the time we open until the time we close. We shut the kitchen down an hour later on home game nights. Guests will come from the game to the restaurant to have dinner or drink at the bar.

Our regular customers are outside when we get here in the morning, especially on Raven's Sunday mornings. The bartenders let some of our regulars in while they set up the restaurant. Everybody wants to get a good seat in front of those sixty-inch flat screen televisions surrounding the bar. There are three screens with different channels going at once. When the Ravens game is on, all three televisions are tuned it. Jaime turns on the outside speakers so people can hear the game as they stroll the Harbor. Some people sit at the amphitheater, listen to the game, and eat lunch.

There are two floors at the Inner Harbor location. We are the only location with two levels, a bar, a sweethearts booth with a chocolate fountain, and two patios. There is a lower level patio and one directly above overlooking Baltimore's beautiful Inner Harbor. We rent out the patios during the holiday seasons for parties. The upstairs balcony has a great view of the fireworks during the holidays with a picturesque view of Federal Hill.

The Fourth of July is booked for the next two years. We have corporate accounts. They have first priority over everyone else. Pete's caters to businesses around downtown. It could be a law office, doctor's office, mayor's office, or even a public or private school. They'll put their orders in on Monday and their orders will go out Tuesday at twelve. Clients have until Thursday to pay their account in full. We also deliver to coffee shops and bakeries around town. Jaime is pretty popular here in the city.

The lower level is where the bar and lounge are. It's popular for the sports fan or if you want to have a drink. There is smoking. We have an open patio and entrance to the Pratt Street Pavilion. The bar stays packed. We only put the best servers and the host on the lower level. You have to be able to greet all of the guests, seat them, and answer the telephone. I stay on the second floor. I am upper management. Jaime likes to keep three managers and two assistants on duty. We need that much help.

Pete's Inner Harbor opened in 1998. Our Annapolis location opened a year later. It was popular in the beginning then during the floods our sales declined. Jaime didn't want to close. He had faith in God, himself, and the business. Jaime, his father (Jaime Sr.), and Van, put a plan into action to save the failing restaurant. Van turned the failing restaurant into an empire. Van brought on a new staff and trained the old staff to keep up with the ever-changing industry. He did not want to fire anybody. He said the staff was not the problem. We conducted intense training and turned everything around.

Van hired four managers and a general manager to overlook the place when he is not there. Van travels from location to location when Jaime cannot.

Jaime's baby is the Harbor. He hired close family, friends, and fraternity brothers and sorority sisters to work here. Jaime does all the baking during the holiday season. He is always in the kitchen. Thanksgiving is his favorite time of year. He's getting his menu together for turkey day. We aren't open on Thanksgiving, but we have specials throughout the week. My favorite is the open-faced turkey sandwich with homemade cranberry sauce, turkey gravy on top of mashed potatoes, stuffing, and green beans. That runs for $14.00.

Everybody likes working with Van. I adore him. Van is the type of manager that lets you go home early when it is slow and tells you to come in later when there is no business. Who does not love a man like that? We work together a lot. He's the only one that does not wreck my nerves. With the upcoming holiday season, we need rational thinkers.

Stephan is my assistant. We grew up together. He was friends with my older sister, Altovise. That is until we began working together and I took the title best friend. Stephan used to work at my real estate office, Bond & Harris & Bond, on Charles Street in the business district downtown answering phones and filing. Basically he did secretarial work. Stephan is a hard worker.

It was the first day of spring and opening day at Oriole Park. Jaime ran a $.25 beer and nickel buffalo wing special.

I asked, "Jaime, is there going to be a limit on how many wings you can order?"

Jaime said, "No, Baby. We good."

The lounge area was filled by 12:00 p.m. When the word got out that the wings were $.25, they flew. The specials were gone by first pitch and we had to turn people away. I refused to seat another person. We could not seat or tend to another customer. On top of all that, there were carry out orders going on. When you have specials in a restaurant and carry out, the staff has to stay in constant communication with one another. If we didn't, that would've been a total disaster.

We love our customers like we love our families. I was offered $100.00 to seat a couple in the bar. I grabbed two seats from the bakery and made sure they were comfortable all night. Don't tell Jaime. I am sure he has done the same though.

Customers were in the lounge standing around drinking beers, eating wings, watching the game, and enjoying the breeze off the water. We were at our wits end. Van asked me to call my sister, Sherri. It was more of a demand rather than asking if I could call her to come and help. I didn't hesitate to call. I was about to fall the fuck out.

I called the office and asked Stephan where Sherri was. He said Sherri left for the day because she had cramps. I wanted to snap her neck. She did not call me and tell me she was leaving for the day. She could've shot a text. Nothing. I asked Stephan could he come down and help us. He said sure. He said that no one had come in and all he had was a few calls. He was doing light filing when I called. I told him that I would pay him for the time he worked. Stephan showed up an hour later ready to work and he stayed until we closed.

Stephan has been here four years. He started off as a host and Jaime promoted him to assistant general manager within six months. No one argued with that. We need someone like Stephan. He's a sweetheart. He listens well and handles conflict without breaking a sweat or those Swarovski studded stiletto nails he rocks.

Our staff is the absolute best. They argue over who has more hours. They all have a strong work ethic and they love Jaime. Jaime gives out the best presents during the holidays and birthdays. Most employers give out gift cards or nothing at all. Jaime gave out iPods one year and management got iPads for work. I haven't seen a damn soul bring theirs back to work or even work on one. We all work on the MacBook on Jaime's desk.

While I was in the office getting register paper, the DJ on the radio said, "There's six to twelve inches of snow expected to fall on the city between tonight and tomorrow morning."

He said he didn't have any additional details because they were coming in by the minute. The DJ added that once he got more information, he would break in.

I hurried out of the office and spoke to Van. Maryland's weather is unpredictable. One week we're wearing sweaters, UGG boots, and coats, and the next day we can wear shorts, flip flops, and a t-shirt.

Now, I will say that it is rare that Baltimore will get a major snowstorm in November. It was eighty degrees last week. We opened the patio and customers were out there in shorts and flip flops eating wings and drinking Stella's while watching the boats come in. There was a cool breeze off the water. The very next day, I pulled out the Bailey Button UGG boots and a thick wool, cowl neck sweater.

Van was in the kitchen having a ball with the cooking crew. I stood next to him and asked had he heard from Jaime? Van looked at his Rolex as if he knew what time the storm would start. He nodded as he wiped the sides of a plate.

I asked again, "Did Jaime call?"

Van shook his head no as he checked his cell phone, which he had within arm's reach.

"I am waiting for him to call."

I exhaled as I looked out on the floor. We had a full restaurant. It didn't look like the customers were concerned about the storm, but I was definitely worried. We have staff that catch the bus. So, while the diners dined on German chocolate cake, thick pieces of homemade sweet potato pie, and sipped coffee, I told the staff to break down and close up. I didn't want anyone to get stuck.

The snow was picking up. There was a pink tint to the sky over the Harbor. The sun was setting while the big, beautiful flakes fell. It was a magnificent sight to see. I let my staff that catch public transportation go home. I hadn't heard if they were shutting down the public transportation system. When it snows, the light rail and subway shut down because they are above ground. Buses stop running. It's a mess. Who wants to risk that?

Van and I were the last to leave as always. I went into the office and updated our answering machine. I called the account holders and the parties scheduled for the next day. Van came into the office and told me to wrap it up because the snow was coming down in buckets and visibility was almost at zero. I logged off and headed out with him. He was tapping his Rolex as we walked down the hall to the kitchen.

Jaime sent out a mass text urging management to close up after I had already made the executive decision to close.

Monica and Red were waiting in the lobby of the Pratt Street Pavilion. I promised them a ride home earlier that evening. I had parked in the Gallery Mall parking garage across the street from the restaurant. I usually valet park, but since it was the middle of the day, I lucked up and got a parking space. I gave Red the keys to my Range Rover.

I told him, "Do not fuck up my car."

Monica and I stood in the hallway of the pavilion waiting for Red to bring the Range Rover. I didn't feel like walking. Monica was pregnant with her second baby. She did not feel like walking either after working twelve hours.

Jaime and I lived in upstate New York for four years. I attended Syracuse while he worked alongside his best friend, Lionel, in his father's five-star Michelin restaurant. I can drive in snow. I didn't learn how to drive until we moved to upstate New York. I can get around if I have to, but I don't want to. In my personal opinion, Baltimoreans cannot drive in the snow.

Upstate New York had the worst winters I'd ever experienced, and I had to get around in the snow because we did not shut down like Maryland.

I trusted Red to make the drive home. Monica sat in the front. I was relaxed in the back. I closed my eyes. I didn't know I was asleep until Red shook me. I asked him could he drop me off at my mother's house and he could take the Range. I was too tired to drive home. He made sure Monica got inside, then he drove fifteen minutes up the street to my mother's house where my baby was waiting for me.

I could hear the bass bumping in the Range as Red pulled off. I made my way up the concrete steps. When I was younger, I ran up and down those concrete stairs like it was nothing. Now, it's a race to see if I make it up six out of the twelve of them.

I put the key in the door. I admired the view of the fresh snow falling over Lake Montebello. It is so beautiful. Quiet. Still. Nothing but the sound of a few cars riding up and down Hillen Road and the snow falling. Have you ever heard snow fall with a hint of wind blowing? It's absolutely the best. The city was covered in a thin coating of snow.

I turned the knob and went inside. I smiled. My heart melted as soon as I looked up. There he was sitting on Mama's lap eating a chocolate chip cookie.

"Hey," I said as I walked into the house.

My baby Jaime's hands flapped up and down like he hadn't seen me in forever. I took my fifteen pound chocolate chip in my arms and kissed his forehead. I whispered that I missed him.

Of course, he said, "Dada."

I exhaled and rolled my eyes.

Mama laughed as she made her way into the kitchen. I followed her.

"You're home earlier than I anticipated," she said as she took a hand towel from the counter and opened the oven.

I sat at the round, wooden table. I did a lot of homework on this table. Altovise would sit on the other side, gossiping. I smiled as I bounced my beautiful baby boy on my knee. This was the best part of my day.

"Yeah," I said as I pulled baby Jaime's shirt over his belly. "Jaime said that we could lock up and go home."

Mama agreed as she removed a tray of freshly baked chocolate chip cookies from the oven. She had a tray cooling on the counter next to a pot of coffee.

"Yup," she said as she sat them down. "They been talking about it all day."

"Is the coffee fresh?"

"I can make another pot."

"No, Ma, I can drink that."

"It's from dinner. I made beef stew and hot buttered cornbread. Ready to eat?" she asked as she went over to her eight-burner stove and grabbed a bowl from her cupboard. "I also made pecan pie that's cooling."

"Thanks, Mama."

I got the last of a dying breed. They don't make Mama's like they used to. And I am so blessed to have my mama.

I've never eaten alone since I had my baby. I propped him on my knee, grabbed his little spoon, and fed him beef stew juice. He yelled at me because I stopped feeding him to grab a few bites for myself. I even crumbled up some cornbread with a little butter and gave it to him. And when it was all gone and he had beef stew all over his chocolate face, his eyelids fluttered, and he fell asleep.

I laughed when his head titled and never moved. His stomach was nice and tight.

I carried my baby boy up to my old bedroom. I flipped the light switch and squinted. Damn. It was bright. Mama must've put a thousand-watt bulb in my lamp. The room was nice and clean. Mama comes in and cleans it every once in a while. The bed was made perfectly like those beds with those sharp corners. I never get the bed like that. All of my trophies and awards from school were still lined up nicely. Mama even had my pom poms from when I was a cheerleader in middle school. I used to run track in high school. I drew a huge crowd cause guys like looking at the girl with the big booty run. I made it to state final and broke my damn ankle. I put on fifty pounds and stopped running. I don't regret giving up running and gaining those fifty extra pounds though.

I laughed as I placed the baby down on the bed. He's so fat, he's not going to roll. And if he falls, he has enough cushion. I headed over to my desk. There was a picture of Jaime and I on a roller coaster at Kings Dominion. I smiled as I held the picture in the silver frame. Tears filled my eyes as I placed the frame down. We had a good time that day. It was my senior trip. He had flown in from Paris just to take me to my prom. He stayed for my senior trip, prom, senior activities, and of course graduation day where he presented me with a car I couldn't drive. I took a lot of pictures. I wanted that moment to last forever. It is something that I will always cherish.

I was the most hated girl on the block because I had a man with money that loved me. He bought me any and everything a girl could possibly dream of. I miss him so much. I miss holding him. I miss his laugh and his pancakes. After all we had been through having this baby and overcoming storms, you'd think we'd be closer. I want my husband here with me. I want to fall asleep listening to his heartbeat. How did we get here?

Chapter Two

IT WAS ALL GOOD JUST A YEAR AGO

Jaime Harris

It was all good just a year ago…

Just like my beautiful wife, I'm still trying to figure out how we got here. Why am I here alone? Why am I sitting here in the dark drinking this alcohol? I miss my baby and my wife dearly. God, it took us what seemed like forever to get here. We were both happy. Well, she was happy. I was being Jaime. All I asked her for was some space. She did not have to give me this much space and leave me. Be careful what you pray for, you just might get it. I am blessed to have a woman like Ashanti in my life. Where did we go wrong? I've been asking myself this for the last year.

I woke up at 5:00 a.m. I ran five miles on the treadmill, five miles on the elliptical, and did another five miles on the bike. There was nothing unusual about that day. I did my same morning routine--shower, coffee, breakfast bar, and out the door by 9:00 a.m. I hopped in the Benz and bumped Jay. I like when I stop at red lights and the girls peep in the car, wave, and giggle like they never seen dick. I kept a straight face. As soon as the light turned, I winked, and pulled off.

I went to work. It was business as usual. I was sick when I left the house, but I did not think my sickness was going to progress as fast as it did. I work around food, so I can't spew germs and get everybody else sick; it's a health risk. I am always on my employees about coming in sick. I have to send them home. They love working with me so much, I have to threaten them with death to send them home. I love what I do. Cooking is in my blood. It is my life. It is my passion. I make love to food. I love my profession so much, it shows. I gravitate to people. They gravitate to me. It's a bond. When you love what you do, it's not work, and the people around you feel it.

I tried to stay away from the kitchen. The prep crew came in at 7:00 a.m. They called me fifty times before I got to the restaurant. I had a huge holiday shipment coming in. They weren't sure what went where.

I said, "Just make it nice and neat. Don't just put shit anywhere. I will handle it when I get in."

My cooks arrive around 10:00 a.m. I would like them there by 9:00 a.m., but they do what they want.

By that time, my manager Belle, Ashanti's aunt, went to the drug store to get me some over-the-counter cough syrup. It soothed my throat just in time for the lunch rush.

I washed my hands and joined my crew. Belle was in charge of the pre-shift five- to ten-minute meeting we have each shift. I expect my management crew to be at the restaurant by 9:00 a.m. We open at 11:00 a.m. When Stephan and Van open, they are usually there by 9:00 a.m., and pre-shift and memos are usually done.

When I open, I usually do the pre-shift meeting, but I was not in the mood. I stayed in the office with tissue up one nostril and the other running like a faucet. This can't be life. I never get sick.

I had a strong crew this morning. Monica is the perfect employee. She can run the restaurant better than me. I thought about making her manager then we got Stephan; he is awesome. He's the reason why I sat out part of the lunch rush. He expedited and did everything I was supposed to do. I wasn't going to hire him at first. He had no experience.

I said, "Shit. I didn't have experience working alongside Lionel in his father's five-star Michelin restaurant. I went with the flow. They gave me a chance."

I gave Stephan a chance because they believed in me. I believe in him.

Gisselle is my assistant manager/trainer. She trains everyone except the cooks. Gisselle started off as a host and worked her way up. She is a feisty, no-nonsense type of chick.

The new employees do not like her. She's worse than I am. I have been told I am the laid back one.

Inner Harbor is the first location I opened after working years in catering and being a personal chef to lawyers, doctors, judges, and politicians in DC. Inner Harbor is my baby. It was my mother's idea to open a location in Annapolis. It was to appeal to the wealthy women in her circle that heard of me but don't want to travel to the city to get good soul food.

When I opened Annapolis, I sent Gisselle there for a week to train. When we revamped the restaurant, she was there as well. I was going to close the Annapolis location due to low sales and the floods, but my family convinced me to keep it open. Especially when the revenue started coming in and I had no choice but to keep it open.

Towson was the third and supposedly final location I opened. The demand was there. Customers used to ask when I was going to get into Towson and grab up some of that property. They were revamping the area and I wanted to get in on the ground floor. I did some in-depth research on properties. I asked Ashanti could she find a building and handle everything.

Towson is a smaller location. Alexis was the general manager until she got pregnant and I promoted Juan. Juan is Monica's husband. I have to watch out for him. He has a lot going on over there with his female staff and I don't mean handing out hours. He's handing out dick. I told him to watch out. There are some pretty ass girls that work there.

I said, "If you're going to fuck with them, fuck with one. You not supposed to fuck with any of them but be careful."

I don't know. I got my own shit going on.

Alexis is the brains. She is the rational one and a free spirit. She's the one you can turn to for advice. She takes a lot of the girls under her wing and guides them. Alexis works down here at the Inner Harbor. She's one of my senior servers. In the kitchen, we have my cousin Red and my man Cecil. Let's not forget my right hand, Van Smith. We went to Morgan State together, we pledged together, and up until my sophomore year, we played football together. I was a beast. They kept bothering me about going into the NFL. I wasn't interested. I wanted to cook. When I got hurt, I celebrated. I was so happy. My leg was fucked up in six places. That was my cue to cook. There were times when I did not want to go out on the field. But I was so good I had no choice but to go out there. I didn't want to waste my talent. My mother was so proud of me. She bragged about me every chance she got. It hurts from time to time, but when you got money it cures everything.

Pete's is increasingly growing in popularity. We stayed busy from 11:00 a.m. until 2:30 p.m. By then, Van clocked in. I asked Stephan could he take over. Stephan said that I didn't look good.

I said, "I don't feel good."

Everybody was talking about the impending snowstorm. I wasn't worried about the storm. I am not a tyrant. I am not going to let my people stay out or come in if it gets out of hand. I called my soon to be ex-wife and told her that I was leaving early. She asked what was wrong. I told her that I had the flu. I did not feel good at all.

"Jaime." Belle called from the kitchen.

I had packed up my duffle bag and was headed out the door when she stopped me.

"Yes," I sniffled.

"What special do you want to run tonight?" she asked.

Belle had a pen and pad ready to take notes. I told her to walk with me. For a big woman, she kept up. I told her to run whatever she felt like because I was going home. We paused. She slapped her hands on her thighs and laughed. I blew her a kiss and left for the afternoon. They can handle it. I believe in them.

When I got home, I took a nice long, hot shower. I did not want to be disturbed. I turned off my phone, turned up Brian McKnight, grabbed a bottle of wine from the cellar, and zoned out. I dressed, started making myself some chicken noodle soup with the freshest ingredients, and relaxed. There is nothing better than quiet time alone. Once the soup was done cooking, I grabbed a bowl and headed to the living room to sit in front of the big screen television.

There was a knock on the door. I exhaled. I pay way too much damn money for someone to just walk up and knock on my door. What happened to the doorman? I sat my soup down on the coffee table and opened the door.

"Hey."

I leaned on the door. I rolled my eyes up in my head. I told her not to show up unannounced. I'm still married.

I never imagined that Ashanti and I would be in this situation. I sat on the couch next to my unexpected guest. She talked about how much she missed me. Her mouth was moving, but I didn't hear anything that was coming out of it. I thought back to a much simpler time when Ashanti and I were together. I hated coming home alone.

I hated this life. I miss her smile. I miss cooking for her. She didn't care what time I got off work or how tired I was, she wanted dinner. One time, she called while I was at the gym and turned my day completely around. Ashanti had that kind of effect on me. I like to stay in shape and whenever I am having a bad day, I work out. It's not easy being in the kitchen with those young dudes. They run circles around me. I have to keep my stamina up. I got to show them I still got it.

I thought back to about a year ago, around the time when Ashanti and I's relationship began to take a turn for the worse. I was on the treadmill getting work in when she called.

"Hey, Baby."

"Hey, Love." I slowed down and hopped off the treadmill.

Before all of this nonsense, Ashanti and I lived out in Owings Mills (a suburb in Baltimore County) in a beautiful gated community with crystal chandeliers and heated marble floors. Our neighbors were football, basketball, and soccer players; actors; actresses; lawyers; and politicians. When they found out that I was a personal chef, they eased their way to my condo and asked could I cater for them or cook personal meals.

"What ya doing?" Ashanti asked. She wanted something. I could hear it in her voice.

"I am working out."

There was a long why didn't you tell me pause and then she asked, "Well, why didn't you tell me?"

I tried not to laugh. I tried getting her to come to the gym. Ashanti plays when she comes to the gym. She is on her phone. She does not take it seriously. I like to work out for at least two hours on Saturday mornings. The gym in the complex is open twenty-four hours. I'll wake her and ask her would she like to come. She'll roll over and say, "Next time." Needless to say, next time never comes. Well, there was that one time when she miscarried. She fell into a slight bought with depression and gained a lot of weight. When she realized that her Chanel boots were a little tight, something had to be done. I'm glad Chanel snapped her out of her sadness. I was all out of resources. She put in the effort and lost enough weight to get into her boots again. I was proud of her. She almost died that week.

"What's for dinner?" Ashanti asked.

She can't be serious. I just worked out for two hours, worked all day, and she wants me to what? "What would you like, Baby?" I asked.

I miss our cute conversations. She made my day. I miss her so much. It is killing me that I cannot call her and talk to her like I used to. Our love was like a fairy tale; it was perfect.

"Ummm, meatloaf, mashed potatoes with garlic, and those glazed carrots you make."

"Sure, Love."

I couldn't resist her smile, her charm, and that body is awesome. Ashanti may have a little weight on her, but she is perfectly proportioned in all the right places. Ashanti makes her pajamas look sexy. She makes a cold look sexy with her hair all over her head.

"What time will you be home?" she asked.

"In a few."

"Okay."

I talked to Ashanti until I got home. I checked the fridge. I had three potatoes. I peeled them and put them in a pot of water with a little salt and butter. I turned the heat down low. While the potatoes cooked, I diced garlic, onion, peppers, and breadcrumbs for the meatloaf. I did not have carrots. I showered really quickly then dressed. I took the potatoes off the eye and let them cool while I hurried to the grocery store to get some carrots. I was a sucker for this woman. I was head over heels in love with her. I would've traveled to the ends of the earth and back for her. And when I got there, purchased what she asked for, and it wasn't the perfect fit or right item, I would've turned around and went right back. She was the love of my life. What happened?

Chapter Three

MEMORIES

I love my piece of chocolate. Jaime is beautiful. He has smooth dark skin, bright beautiful white teeth, and a smile that will light up the room. Jaime recently turned forty but he has the body of a twenty-five-year-old. He has to keep in shape in order to do what he does. If he doesn't keep up, he will fall between the cracks.

"Jaime," I called out as I entered our condo.

Jaime was at the counter whipping the mashed potatoes like they owed him money. I love watching him cook. He's a perfectionist. The homemade gravy was in a separate pot, simmering on very low heat. The carrots were perfectly glazed over with brown sugar and honey on the first eye, and the meatloaf was cooling. I could not wait to eat.

"Yes, Love."

He's very neat and cleans as he goes along. There's not a dirty dish in the sink.

"You should make me a cake."

His deep dark brown eyes widened. I laughed. He looked away from me and continued dinner. "Ashanti Harris," he giggled, "stop playing with me."

"No, for real."

I am a sweets eater. I love cakes, cookies, and pies.

"Make me a carrot cake."

I had been craving carrot cake for days. I just didn't have the nerve to ask him to make it because it takes up so much time.

And just like that he says, "Shred up the carrots and I got you."

I placed my Louis Vuitton messenger bag on the granite kitchen counter along with my keys. I removed my pink pea coat, laid it across the kitchen table, and gathered the bowls and mixers for him.

I asked, "Do you have the ingredients?"

He nodded as he wiped sweat from his brow. He instructed me to get all of the ingredients from the cupboard as well as the appliances he would be using. It's fun being married to a chef.

I had a few minutes before dinner would be done. I went to use the bathroom, wash my hands, and change into something comfortable. When I returned to the kitchen, Jaime had laid the freshly rinsed carrots out on the counter next to the food processor. I shredded the carrots and measured out all the ingredients he said he needed.

I went to the bedroom, sat at my vanity, and grabbed the warm vanilla sugar lotion. I squirted a little on my hands and rubbed it in.

As I was rubbing my hands together, my phone rang. I picked it up and answered.

"Hello."

"Hey, Love."

It was my older sister Altovise (pronounced: Al-toe-vise). She was the popular one growing up. Still is. Kinda. Sorta. My sister never worked a day in her life. Men took care of her. I didn't have that advantage until I met Jaime. It was never my intention to meet a man with money. It happened by chance. My sister on the other hand seeks out money. You have to have a certain amount of money to get with her. She'll let you know at hello.

"Hey."

"Where is Jaime?"

"He's in the kitchen cooking dinner. What's up?"

"Monica."

I laughed. "What about Monica?" I asked. I stood from the vanity and walked over to the balcony overlooking Owings Mills. It was a beautiful sight. Trees and greenery as far as the eye can see. And it was peaceful.

Monica is Altovise's stepdaughter. I think she knows something about my sister.

"She needs to get it together. She's pregnant."

"Oh really?" I asked as I closed the drapes and walked out of the bedroom.

My sister has never been able to bear children. She has been pregnant several times, but her pregnancies never go full term. My heart goes out to her, but she has got to cool it when someone gets pregnant.

Jaime and I suffered a miscarriage six months ago. We were looking forward to becoming parents, but my pregnancy only lasted long enough to make me sick and fall into a deep depression. My hair fell out. I didn't want to go on living. I gained a ton of weight. I didn't look like Ashanti and I damn sure as hell didn't feel like Ashanti. Mama took me to church and prayed over me. I just didn't want to do anything but cry. It felt like someone had dangled pregnancy in my face, snatched it away, then laughed as they were walking away with my baby.

"And I know she is going to ask Chuck for money."

Altovise went on and on about Monica. Chuck and Altovise have been married for going on twenty years. Altovise's ex-best friend, Karen, used to be married to Chuck. People can say what they want but that's the reason why Monica does not like Altovise. I also think there is something else going on over there, but I try to mind my own business. My sister on the other hand doesn't.

Altovise and Karen were sorority sisters in college. Karen lived on Tivoly Avenue and went to Mergenthaler High School. Her trade was cosmetology. Altovise was too damn smart for her own good, she went to Western High School for girls.

Karen used to braid my hair. I loved how she did it. No one can braid my hair like Karen. We were tight, almost like sisters. Karen lived with us while she was pregnant with Monica. When Monica was born, Chuck left his parents' house and moved his family into an apartment over in east Baltimore.

Karen and Chuck were madly in love. They were always at the parties and cookouts we had at the house. Karen used to make banana pudding that would knock your socks off. Whenever she makes that banana pudding, Monica brings it in to me. Karen sent me a PM on Facebook a week ago asking how the business and Mama was. I said everything was well. That was the end of that. I don't think she wants to come around because of the Altovise and Chuck situation.

Monica's fiancé is Juan Ortiz. His mother, Lupe, makes a damn good banana pudding as well. Lupe is a good-hearted woman. She does not like Altovise, and to be honest, I do not blame her. My sister can work a nerve. Lupe said Altovise is in Monica and Juan's business too much. I agree. I told my sister to stop getting in Monica's affairs. Altovise does not like Chuck and Monica's relationship.

I said, "Altovise, that is his child. You cannot stop a father from loving his daughter. And you damn sure as hell can't stop a daughter from loving her father. You know how much we love Daddy."

Jaime told me that Altovise was cheating on Chuck with one of the dope boys from around the way. Altovise is best friends with Tita Lewis. He is the Bishop at my mother's church and he's married to Lupe's cousin, Jillian. Jillian does not like Altovise. If my sister would keep her mouth and nose out of people's business, they would like her. She acts as if she does not care that folk don't like her. It's like the older she gets the worse she gets, and no one wants to be around her.

Jillian thought that Tita and Altovise were having an affair. I did too. My sister tells me that she smokes weed with Tita. I asked her why she was smoking weed with him when she knows he's married. She laughed and told me to grow up.

Jillian has asked me on several occasions if Tita and Altovise are having an affair.

I said, "I don't know."

I thought Tita was gay. My sister has a slew of gay male friends. When they told me that Tita was getting married, I said, "To what man?" My mouth hit the floor when I found out he was marrying Jillian. Tita and Altovise were always friends. Altovise and Jillian used to be friends. Then again, look at her and Karen.

Anyway, my sister and the Bishop smoke weed together. They are always getting high and going out. Personally, I don't think Tita makes enough money for Altovise to leave her husband or creep with. The only thing that's going on between them is smoking weed and gossiping.

So, dude that Altovise is or was cheating with has two children by a friend of Monica's. They went to high school together. The baby mother called and told Monica that her baby father was seen with Altovise. Jaime said the same thing. Jaime said that Van saw Altovise and the dude at the movies. Jaime said that Stephan said that Altovise and the boy was down at Pete's hugged up in the corner making out and feeding one another. Gisselle said she saw the guy driving Altovise's Lexus with a girl in the passenger's seat that wasn't his baby mama. I'm not surprised at anything that any nigga do in Baltimore. It's typical Baltimore hood shit. Ask anyone. News spreads fast in Pete's. Don't sneeze.

Monica told Chuck. From what I gather, Chuck did not say anything to Altovise about it. That's what my husband told me. I am waiting for my sister to tell me something.

So, while she's on this phone acting like she's the innocent one, I am going to finish telling you what my husband told me. My husband did not grow up in the city, but he knows everybody because of his cousin Red. He's another fine ass red ass man with green eyes. The girls love him. Anyway, Altovise and Tita went to get some weed from Red. Apparently, Red was not around. He was probably out fucking up somebody's happy home. But that's not any of my business. He gets around. These women would not be sleeping with him if he wasn't fine with that long twelve-inch horse dick I heard about.

The dude's name is Wishbone or Fishbone. I don't know. Word is he had been eyeing my sister for a minute. My sister is gullible as hell. She let the dude drive her truck, she gave him money, and she took him on trips. I don't know what's wrong with her. And you know people in the hood talk. Why would you jeopardize what you have for this dope boy? So, I guess you know what happens next. She gets pregnant. And for the first time in her adult life, she makes it past the first trimester, but she does not want to keep the baby. So, she gets an abortion because she didn't know who the baby father was. She told me that Chuck didn't want no baby and she was too old. So, Altovise's girlfriends were running around

Baltimore telling people that Altovise got an abortion because she didn't know who the baby father was. Why was I the last to find out? And as far as she is concerned, I still don't know shit about her affair. My sister should have told me something about it instead of me hearing secondhand shit from people that don't like me.

My sister knows better. I wish she would've used better judgment. She told the girls that his dick was so good she could not let him go. Okay, how about this, stop fucking dudes you don't know. The baby mama, Stephanie, used to work at Pete's until she got pregnant for a fourth damn time. Girl, when are you going to learn that man is not going to stay with you? I don't care how many babies he puts in you. He constantly disrespects you and brings home diseases.

Altovise always complains about Monica. Monica is the best server Jaime has, and she can cook if she has to. When Jaime left to tend to business at another location, Monica closed down the Inner Harbor location, and she opened the next day. On game day, she pulls in the crowds and makes money. Jaime loves her. He said he doesn't know what he would do without her. He was thinking about making her a supervisor. Now that she is pregnant, I don't know how that is going to go over. I'm not mentioning any of this to Jaime. As far as I know, Monica is not pregnant.

♥

After dinner, I went straight to bed. As soon as my head hit the pillow, I went right to sleep. I had an enormous headache after talking to my sister. Jaime said I shouldn't take things with her so seriously. I don't understand her. I woke up at 3:00 the next morning and went straight to the kitchen to get a slice of carrot cake. Jaime had fallen asleep on the couch. He looked so peaceful, I didn't want to disturb him.

I turned on the kitchen light. I was so excited. My eyes went straight to the crystal cake and cupcake stand Jaime's mom gifted us last year on our wedding anniversary. I died a little when she sent the package from Kirkland's wishing us a happy anniversary, and I was shocked when I opened the Williams-Sonoma box addressed from her. I couldn't wait to get the first slice, but the cake was so pretty I didn't want to slice it.

Jaime's mother was evil. She vacationed in hell. Satan was afraid of her. They knew each other well. Ice did not melt in her mouth. She could kill you with looks and those glares would make you want to toss holy water on her. Evil came home to roost and her name was Clairess Harris.

The gift was for Jaime. She sent numerous crystal cake and cupcake stands to several of his locations as well. Jaime opened Towson and she sent three. The Towson location does not have a bakery. The desserts are made at the Harbor location then Felix drives them with Marcia the bakery manager over to Towson.

When the sweethearts booth downtown got a make-over with new baking appliances, she made it known that she sent the crystal cake and cupcake stands. They fit in perfectly with the Harbor location. My mother-in-law was extra fancy. She was a black republican. Not that there is anything wrong with a black republican. She was wealthy. She was raised within an elite crowd of wealthy blacks in DC. She could never relate to people like me. We are from two different worlds. We had one thing in common, our love for Jaime. My mother-in-law was a stuck-up ass bitch. I could not stand her.

I remember one time when Jaime and I took a week-end off and stayed inside. It was cold and rainy. He thought it would be a good idea to cook dinner, so he made fried chicken, a big pot of Navy beans with pigs feet and ham slices, mile high biscuits, and chocolate cake for dessert. Mama and Papa came. Jaime Sr. and his new woman were there too. He said she was an associate at his firm. Yeah right. He's another one that can't keep his dick in his pants. That young girl couldn't keep her hands off his old ass. Jaime's dad is fine, but he's too generous with the dick.

My aunt Belle even showed up after work. Jaime also invited his mother.

Jaime's father said, "You know she is not going to slum it with us."

We had a good laugh. You could see the hurt in Jaime's face. His mother hurt him. He couldn't help meeting and falling in love with me. He couldn't help wanting to cook for a living. She said it's manual labor but it's not manual labor when it's something you love. And when Jaime cooks, that love shows all over his face.

I overheard him at work the day before the dinner telling Belle that he could not wait to talk to Mama. Jaime always said that he wanted a relationship with his mother. He said that he wished his mother was welcoming just like my family welcomed him. Well, Jaime's mother went to Aruba with some friends and got back the morning of the dinner. When she touched down, she called him and asked could he come pick her up from the airport. He was so excited. He was childlike as he bounced around the restaurant smiling and laughing. He couldn't wait to see her. Before he left, he asked her would she like to come and have dinner. She said no. His mood changed. I had to pull him into the office and tell him to get a grip.

I said, "Just because your mother ruined your day, doesn't mean you have to ruin ours."

He invited her to Las Vegas. She said no. He tried to include her in everything, but she said no every time. She didn't say, "Let me think about it or let me check my book."

Instead, she would ask, "Who is going? Who is paying?"

And when Jaime told her, she'd say, "Of course you're paying."

Does it matter? You said no. You do not want to participate in anything. I don't get in it. Mrs. Harris has never stepped into Pete's Inner Harbor. She's only been to Pete's Annapolis with her snotty ass friends for tea and biscuits. Jaime put tea and biscuits on the menu for brunch. What the hell? We are a soul food restaurant. Put some sausage gravy on that shit and the masses will gobble it up. Jaime knows I do not care for her. He talks about it. I listen. I don't indulge. If she was on fire, I wouldn't piss on her.

Although she was gorgeous, she was the worst human being on the planet. How could something so evil and vile produce the exact opposite? Jaime is nothing like his mother.

The weekend before Jaime and I got married, his mother called and asked would I like to come to dinner? She said it was called a mingling of the families. It was a chance for us to get to know one another before the festivities.

I was already under severe stress. My shoulder length tresses had fallen out from the stress of planning my wedding. There was a lot going on and it felt like I couldn't get ahead. I was flattered. I didn't mind stopping my life to enjoy some quality time with my future mother-in-law. I just knew we were going to get to know one another and discuss the wedding. Jaime was happy. It was a joyous time.

It dawned on me that she did not know any of my family. How was she going to invite anyone, and she knows no one? Jaime said I was overthinking everything and I needed to chill. I was confused. How were we going to have a meet and greet and she didn't know my family? Jaime was busy opening the restaurant. He reassured me that everything would be taken care of. I believed my man and went along with it. I was swamped at work, so I didn't have time to check in with my family to see if they were even extended an invite.

Sunday rolled around and to be totally honest, Jaime and I were so busy that we forgot about the party. He came into the bedroom around 8:00 a.m. that morning and said a team of girls were coming in at 9:00 a.m. to make me extra beautiful. I was so excited. I got up, showered, and lounged around in my white robe eating fresh fruit, cheese, and croissants while sipping champagne from a flute filled with Moët & Chandon. Shortly after I got comfortable, the stylist and her team arrived with champagne and chocolate-dipped strawberries, along with the prettiest dresses I've ever seen in my life. I tried on five. I chose the moss-colored Vera Wang gown; the stylist said the other dresses were mine, and paid for in full. The stylist also had a nail technician, hair stylist, and makeup artist to finish my look. I also got my first pair of Jimmy Choo shoes.

I was flabbergasted. Jaime said I looked like a million dollars. There was a jeweler as well. I could pick out a diamond tennis bracelet, matching necklace, and diamond pinky ring. I had on a million dollars in jewelry. I needed a security guard. Once I was all dolled up, I did not feel comfortable. I told Jaime that I was out of my element.

A stretch limo with more chocolate treats and champagne inside drove us down to Mrs. Harris' estate on the Eastern Shore. Jaime got a phone call from his father on our way down. It was no surprise that his father was not going to be in attendance.

As soon as we entered the oasis, everyone screamed surprise. They applauded and snapped pictures while hugging and kissing on Jaime. He was happy. I didn't know those people. I didn't see any of my family members. I was heartbroken. The servers greeted Jaime and I with tall glasses of Moët & Chandon Dom Pérignon white gold. His mother made this long ass speech. I was uncomfortable and it showed in the pictures I received almost two years later. Then the bitch had the nerve to repeat the speech in French. My eyes widened. Everyone thought it was so great. I was pissed. I ran through two glasses of Moët. The server stood next to me with the bottle because I said don't move. This was going to be a long ass night.

Jaime and I mingled with the crowd. The room was full of people who were strangers to the both of us. When I realized that my family was not coming, tears welled up in my eyes. Jaime pulled me out into the garden which looked like the Garden of Eden. Then again, it can't be the Garden of Eden if it is owned by the spawn of Satan.

"What's wrong, Baby?"

"No one is here."

"I know love," he said as he pulled me close and danced with me.

I giggled. She had a violinist playing near the door of the garden. This was too much for me. "She don't know your family."

I broke away from Jaime. I asked him who did he know. He stood there like a deer caught in headlights as if his black ass had seen a damn ghost. "See."

Dinner was served. We sat down at this long ass table with white linen, tall glasses, and cutlery on both sides. Jaime said to work from the outside in. His mother sat at the head of the table and asked was there a problem? The table looked down at me. Jaime smiled and shook his head no. She knew I had no idea what the fuck I was doing. She knew I was out of my element with this formal setting. We do not have formal settings at my ghetto ass family cookout. We have a paper plate, a napkin, and a plastic fork. We don't have a soup spoon, knife, salad fork, salad knife, beverage spoon, dinner knife, and so the fuck on.

That night, we had chilled peach soup with fresh goat cheese and oysters Rockefeller for apps, glazed duck with vegetables for dinner, ricotta pound cake cupcakes with ricotta frosting for dessert, and coffee. The men had brandy while the women stayed inside and sipped hot apple cider with long cinnamon sticks.

At the end of the evening, my soon to be mother-in-law presented Jaime and I with money for wedding preparations and she also gave us a five-day, four-night honeymoon on the islands of Bora Bora.

She said, "You must travel there at least once in your lifetime."

Then she cut her slanted eyes over to me and said, "Jaime has been twice."

I wanted to die.

The next day, I went to work and told Sherri and Elliott all about it. They laughed. They said they could not with Clara. I had to correct them and tell them her name was Clairess. Elliott laughed and said, "Oh yeah. Clara is the cow."

So, as the day went by, I got a surprise visit. It was my mother-in-law. I didn't know she traveled down to these parts. She wore a long, floor-length mink and her makeup was flawless. Her hair and nails were done to perfection. She had on six-inch heels, her Louis Vuitton bag was on her shoulder, and she wore huge black frames. She was absolutely gorgeous. She was also mean as fuck for no fucking reason.

I wanted to hug her and tell her, "It's going to be okay. Who hurt you?"

She said, "Ashanti, darling. I am so sorry that I did not invite your family."

It was so fake. She went on to say she thought they would've been uncomfortable. You don't say. She asked if I had a good time.

I smiled and said, "Grand."

She said, "Good."

I wanted to claw her damn rich eyes out. That sorry ass apology didn't make up the fact that she did not invite my family to the party. Bitch, go on! The door!

Everybody pray.

Chapter Four

SOUTHERN HOSPITALITY

I cannot believe I ate four slices of carrot cake and was thinking about eating a fifth. I drank all the milk. I needed to get some damn sleep and a cup of coffee. I had a busy day ahead.

"What are you doing?" Jaime asked as he strolled in the kitchen like it was a quarter to noon. He looked at the cake and shook his head.

"Were you going to save me a slice, Ashanti?" he asked as I handed him the knife.

"Look like it's been licked on." He laughed as he took the knife and sliced up a couple slices.

"Ain't nobody gonna eat it but us," I said as I relaxed over the island. Jaime took his free hand and smacked my bottom.

I giggled.

"You a mess," he said. "I told a few people I was making it."

"So, you already planned to make it?"

"No. You asked me."

"Well," I was dumbfounded. "You... you said you were making it for me," I added with my right brow in the air.

Jaime tossed his hands up.

"I can't with you," he laughed. "Are you the only one I'm supposed to cook for?" he asked as he inched closer until we were face to face.

I planted a huge kiss on his soft full lips.

"Is that your solution to everything?" he asked as he wrapped his arms around my waist. I nodded slowly and shoved my tongue down his throat.

Jaime's cooking reminds me of down south cooking. Mama used to take us down to South Carolina for the summers and holidays. Altovise and I didn't want to go because we wanted to hang out with the bad boys. I'm glad my mother sent us down south for the summers. One summer, I left thirteen and came back fourteen. While I was down south that summer, a few of my girl-friends got pregnant, a few other friends went to jail, and I lost a friend to gun violence. Mama knew going down south during the summers would be better for me and my siblings. It kept us out of harm's way.

We stayed with Aunt Gussie. Belle took the entire summer off just to spend time with Gussie. Her house wasn't the best, but it sat on a couple acres of land in the middle of nowhere. Altovise said it was the colored sec-tion of the state. Aunt Gussie used to make homemade carrot cake that tasted a lot like my husband's. Or should I say my husband's carrot cake tastes similar to my aunt's cake. It took me back to the days when life was easy and simple and free--waking up at noon, going to the waterhole, and spending the day by the water with your friends until it was time for lunch.

Aunt Gussie made golden brown fried chicken fried in lard, mile high biscuits, and pinto beans with fat back and iced tea. The iced tea was so sweet. Altovise said it was diabetic iced tea. One sip and you'll end up with sugar and on insulin. Aunt Gussie didn't care. She made sure our bellies were full of that good home cooking. Elliott and I enjoyed every bit. Altovise used to joke a lot but she loved it more than all of us.

You could smell Aunt Gussie's food down the road. The kids used to say, "Aunt Gussie cooking. Food done!"

I told Jaime about my aunt. She was getting up there in age by the time he had come around and she wasn't cooking as much as she used to. We were sad. We loved going down south and hearing stories and singing songs while cooking. I learned a lot from my aunt about family time, love, and food.

Mama said that the cancer had spread. Aunt Gussie didn't want to go to a hospice. She wanted to die at home, so the family made her last days comfortable. I had to make the trip. Jaime was all for it.

Mama said it was only a matter of time. Mama had been saying it was only a matter of time for over a year. I don't know if they misdiagnosed my aunt or what, but she held on. Aunt Gussie always said God has the final say. She was the type that never showed her feelings, but she loved the Lord. Nothing ever bothered her. If you

47

wanted her, she was never far away. She was always sitting in the front room, close to a radio, listening to gospel music with the Bible in her hand. She only moved to make breakfast, lunch, dinner, and plant in her garden. She moved slow but she burned in the kitchen right until the end.

Jaime watched her like she was one of those fancy chefs he learned from. As I sat and reminisced, eating my cake with my love, I wondered did my aunt give him the recipe? The cakes are so similar. Jaime's cakes are lighter. Aunt Gussie's cake was dense almost like cornbread, but it was just as good as Jaime's. Mama said Aunt Gussie put cream cheese icing on her cake. It did not taste like cream cheese.

Jaime and I stayed with Aunt Gussie for two days. Jaime had to get back home to run the restaurant. I didn't want to leave her. She cooked breakfast, lunch, and dinner for us the entire time we were there. On the day we arrived, an F1 tornado tore through the county. I thought it was the end of the world. Jaime and I were driving, eating snacks, and all of a sudden it got dark.

I said, "What in all that is holy is going on down here?"

Jaime laughed as the EBS came across the radio and said that there was a tornado warning and that we should take cover. He said we were two minutes away from Aunt Gussie's.

We pulled up on the dirt road. Aunt Gussie had her white sheets blowing in the wind. Jaime and I had pulled up just in time to help her take down the sheets. She was frail but she had enough strength in her to do simple tasks. Once we were inside, she told us to go in the basement and wait for the tornado to pass over. Once the storm passed over (it seemed like an eternity, but it was only five minutes), the sun came up, the sky was clear blue, and a rainbow appeared. I stood out on the porch and admired God.

Aunt Gussie had prepared a magnificent meal for Jaime and me. She made cabbage with ham, potatoes, cornbread, macaroni and cheese, rice and gravy, fried chicken, and lima beans. Jaime's eyes were huge when he saw the enormous feast she had prepared. When she pulled those mile high biscuits out of the oven, I wanted to faint. I hadn't had biscuits like that since I was a teenager.

If Aunt Gussie was tired, she sat down. If she was sleepy, she went to sleep. I watched her the entire time she slept. Jaime asked me if I was coming to bed. I said nope. We sat there and watched her all night.

She woke up and screamed, "What the hell y'all doing in my bed?"

She had to have felt us there throughout the night. I heard her get up three times to use the bathroom. She even asked Jaime to help her out of the bed and over to the bathroom.

She said, "Wait outside the door just in case I need you."

He said, "Sure, Aunt Gussie."

Aunt Gussie passed shortly after we left. I don't think we were out of South Carolina when we got word of her passing. Jaime said she held on for us. I cried all the way home. Mama called an hour after we got on the road and asked were we with the family? I said no, we had left.

Aunt Gussie's oldest daughter, Avery, called Jaime and said, "My mother has something for you."

He asked what it was.

She said, "It's in the mail. Take care of it, please. It meant a lot to my mother and our family."

I was jealous.

The pecan pie recipe my mother had been wanting all her life went to Jaime. My grandmother's peach cobbler, fried apple pie, and her mile high buttermilk biscuits recipe passed down from generation to generation also went to Jaime. He sends Aunt Gussie's daughter's a percentage of the sales quarterly. The last I heard, Jemma was traveling with her daughter, Tammy. Avery still lives down south. She sold Aunt Gussie's house, moved to Atlanta, and opened a hair salon.

Since Aunt Gussie passed, everybody goes to Jemma's house for the holidays. I wish I could make the commute. Monica and her fiancé Juan go down there all the time. If I could, I would. Jemma's as sweet as the pecan pie her mother used to make.

So, we're sitting eating cake and talking, then all of a sudden Jaime wants to get freaky. How did we get here? I'm not upset about it though. Jaime ran his fingers up and down my spine sending shivers through my body. How could I love someone so much that it hurt? And how could we end up where we are now? I needed answers. I needed help. I needed my husband.

He picked me up and placed me on the counter. As he kissed my neck, I reached for his boxers. I eased my hands down the front and found what I was looking for. He moaned. As I was about to put my lips around that sweet anaconda that was crying, I stuck out my tongue as a little dribble fell from the head. He was excited. There was a knock on the door. Jaime and I paused.

He told me not to stop. I did as I was told and ran my fingers up and down his shaft. The knocks got louder.

"I am going to have that doorman fired."

"Baby, he's probably asleep," I said as I jumped up from the counter. "Maybe they got the wrong house," I continued as I followed Jaime to the front door.

"Go in the bedroom and lock the door."

I paused and placed my hands firmly on my hips. "Are you serious?"

Jaime shook his head as he reached for the door and opened. "Nigga."

It was his cousin Felix. I rolled my eyes and went to bed. For Felix to show up this time of the morning is never good. Felix showing up at any time is never good. What did Jay-Z say? "You can pay for school but you can't buy class"? That's Felix. For Felix to come from a family with money, he acts like he started from the bottom.

He's always talking about the struggle. He knows nothing about the struggle except struggling to get out of the bed in the morning and making something out of his ratchet life. Everything has been handed to that boy. He is spoiled just like Jaime. His mother never lifted a finger her entire life. His father is a lawyer. I don't have time for rich people problems. They don't have problems like you and me.

"Ashanti."

I don't know what time Jaime came to bed. When I went to bed, the *Anderson Cooper 360* rebroadcast was on. And before I knew it, Anderson was watching me.

"Ashanti." That was not my husband shaking me. "I got some food stamps."

I opened my eyes. Jaime was in the bathroom cracking up. I didn't find anything funny. What does a man with a damn rich ass family know about food stamps? He ought to be ashamed, but this is Felix we are talking about. I told him to go talk to Altovise. She goes down to the Northeast Market and buys stamps. I had no words for that fool. The fact that he was in my room at 7:00 in the morning talking to me about food stamps blew me away. His breath was on a hundred thousand million trillion. It burned my nose hairs.

"He is leaving with you, right?"

Jaime walked out of the bathroom dressed and ready for work. He nodded as he sprayed a little Jean Paul Gaultier on his wrist. I sat up.

"Want to have lunch with me today?" he asked.

I nodded as I pulled the comforter up to my chest. Jaime walked over to the bed.

"I love you."

"I love you too," he said while kissing my lips.

"See you later, Love."

"Bye, Love."

I woke up a little after ten. I made myself a bagel with salmon cream cheese spread, orange juice, and coffee. I watched *Kathie Lee & Hoda* while I did my hair. They give me life in the morning. I would love to sit and have a glass of wine with them.

I took a shower, dressed, and headed to the Starbucks in the lobby of my complex. Jaime said the only reason why he bought the condo was because of the Starbucks. He knows I love it. I will admit that it took a while to adjust to being with someone with money. I really don't need to be involved in the real estate business or working those long, hard hours at Pete's. Jaime has told me plenty of times I don't have to lift a finger.

My family has a strong work ethic, except Altovise. My mother owns a popular bakery called Just Desserts Sweets in the business district downtown not too far from my real estate agency.

Mama's sticky buns are just as popular as the Baltimore crab cake. She is up at dawn with her staff kneading dough, taking orders, ringing up customers, and serving the best coffee, teas, sandwiches, and soups for the hungry lunch crowds.

If Mama runs out of sweets, she will send people to Jaime's. All of Mama's desserts are prepared fresh each day and they are mouthwatering.

Jaime and Mama work hand in hand. Mama's bakery is closed on Saturdays and Sundays, so he uses her bake room on those days. The bake staff comes in at 3:00 in the morning. Jaime is expanding his bakery. He's currently negotiating with the landlords in the pavilion. Until he gets his space, he will continue to use Mama's bake room.

He has a few corporate accounts around the city. He makes his specialty cakes and pies and sells them to small coffee shops and bakeries. It's something he did not want to get into at first so I told him he needs to hire someone to take care of that. But, he says he can do it. We shall see.

During the holidays, Jaime sells chocolate chip cookies and chocolate chip cookie cakes. It's the only time he sells cookies. He has some accountholders and friends that he will make them for, but you have to talk a lot of money for him to think about it. He says cookies are a pain, especially his chocolate chip cake.

The sweethearts booth is a popular hangout space for kids after school. When 3:30 p.m. hits, most of us run because they come in for the cookies and milk. Jaime stocks up on cartons of milk so they can take their sweets to go. They are good kids, but it's irritating to have them in the bar area. I have to put them out. They buy their milk and sweets then have the nerve to sit at the bar. Excuse me.

One of our regulars came in looking for something different for her son's birthday party. She said she didn't want cake. Aunt Belle suggested the peanut butter and jelly pie pockets. Jaime laughed and nodded. I stood there with my right brow in the air. We read each other's minds from time to time. He knew I was thinking money.

The client laughed and asked what it was. Aunt Belle told her about Jaime's fried peanut butter and jelly pocket sandwich that he makes for us. It's not on the menu but the staff loves it. Jaime told her to come in the next day and he would make a batch for her.

That Sunday, she came in with a $500.00 check to be distributed between the bakers. That was a $100.00 tip for each of them. She said the pockets were such a success that she ran low and had to cut them in half. The kids fell in love. Jaime still caters that little boy's parties. Well, he's a grown adult now. His mother brought in ten clients and that ten bought another ten and that ten, well, Jaime had to open another Pete's and expand the bakery.

Over the past couple of years, especially at Thanksgiving, the peanut butter and jelly pie sells out. The kids come in daily to get a peanut butter and jelly pocket. One of the kids told Jaime to start selling milk and orange juice in the morning. Per their request, we open the bakery at 7:00 a.m., close down at 10:00 a.m., and reopen at 12:00 p.m. It's a success. We also serve the peanut butter and jelly pie with a scoop of ice cream on the dessert menu. There is a full, half, pocket size, and half pocket size option. Customers have been calling in orders for the holidays as early as October. Last year, a local news channel did a feature on our peanut butter and jelly pie. Jaime took the news crew and journalist to the bakery and showed them how the pie is made, he also sent pies back to the station.

I work the day before Thanksgiving at the sweethearts booth because of the overwhelming success. Aunt Belle takes the orders starting in October. When we first started our "Thanks for Giving" half off dessert sale, it was just Belle and myself working. Over the years, it has gotten huge; people line up at 6:00 in the morning to get half off cakes, pies, and dessert treats.

I go in at 6:00 a.m. I do not leave until 4:00 or 5:00 in the evening. You cannot purchase desserts the day before the holiday. The only orders going out are those that pre-ordered. You can order up until that Sunday. We have to cut it off or we will never get out of Pete's.

We also serve chocolate covered cherries, chocolate dipped strawberries, orange slices, pineapples, and cashews. The cashews are my favorite. Jaime made those for me when we first started dating. That's how he won my heart.

Everyone asks Jaime where the name sweethearts booth came from. He always says, "It came from Ashanti because she's my sweetheart."

It's all the treats Jaime made for me to get to my heart. He should've put pancakes on the menu cause his blueberry pancakes are life.

"There's my love."

I entered the restaurant with my dark shades on and my Chanel purse on my shoulder. I was wearing my diamond earrings, bracelet, and necklace, and my hair was flowing down my back. Jaime wrapped his arms around my waist and kissed my forehead.

"Hungry?" he whispered in my ear.

He had a table for two set up in the corner away from everyone else.

"Of course," I said as we slid into the booth. I placed my purse next to me.

"Do you know what you want?"

"Macaroni and cheese and meatloaf."

Jaime exhaled. "What's up with you and meatloaf?"

Jaime slid out of the booth. I asked him where he was going. He said he was coming back and blew a kiss as he walked away. I told him to put in an order for a crab cake appetizer, a glass of wine, and two baskets of butter bread. He nodded as I made myself comfortable in the booth. I managed to cross my legs and place my hand on the table, admiring my perfectly shaped red nails and the ring shining on my finger. Jaime upgrades my ring for every year we've been together. I managed to get ten carats. I was a good wife. When I gave birth to Jaime, I got a yellow, nine carat, canary diamond ring. I got a carat for each pound the baby weighed. I still have all of my jewelry.

Gisselle walked over to the booth, along with Jaime, with our food. Jaime slid into the booth as she placed the crab cake mini's between us. I grabbed the plate. She giggled and asked if we would like anything else. We shook our heads no. Gisselle walked away.

Jaime moved closer and whispered in my ear, "It's been a while since we've been this close."

He picked up a fork, sliced into the crab cake, and fed me.

"Awwwwwwwwwwwww!!!!!"

Jaime lowered his head into his chest. I snickered. It was Altovise.

"Who let you in?" Jaime asked as he wiped the corners of his mouth.

"Can I have lunch with my love?" Altovise asked.

"No," I laughed.

Altovise placed her Tory Burch purse on the table and slid into the booth.

"I thought you were going to get your hair done," she said to me.

Altovise grabbed the basket of bread and finished it off.

"I had other things to do," I said as I dug into the crab cake. "I straightened it myself. You like?" Altovise nodded.

"It's okay," she said as she grabbed my glass of wine and sipped.

Jaime sat there and shook his head in playful disgust.

Then Jasmine, Jaime's assistant, sashayed into the restaurant like she owned the place. All eyes fell on her shapely body. That girl's got some dangerous ass curves.

The kind that are God given. Dr. Miami can't perform that kind of miracle. She's blessed by the Father, the Son, and the Holy Spirit. Jasmine wore huge dark frames, high heels, and an attitude. Her attitude stinks like some sour ass milk or Gouda cheese that sat out for too long. You can smell it as soon as she enters the room. Her attitude is so foul, she spits fire. She's mean and dangerous, but girl has style. I do not like her. My husband's attention shifts whenever she enters the room. Jasmine is a beautiful girl. She has a thing for my husband and does not like me at all. I was against hiring her because she had an attitude from day one.

Gisselle said, "It shouldn't matter about her attitude, we need someone."

I said, "We do not hire someone just to have someone."

The only person Jasmine interacts with is Jaime. Jaime thinks the shit is cute. I find it disgusting. I told him, "The bitch has a thang for you."

He laughed and told me to stop playing. My name is Ashanti Harris not Stevie Wonder. I'm not blind.

Altovise cleared her throat as Jaime slid from the booth. I lost my love. Where was my love going? We were having lunch. I looked up. I tried to hold back the tears. I excused myself. I went to the bathroom and cried. I never cried so hard before in my life.

"Knock knock."

I opened the door and was face to face with my sister. She joined me in the stall. She held me so close. I couldn't breathe but it didn't matter cause I wanted to die.

Chapter Five

WHO DO YOU LOVE?

I stepped out of the bathroom. Altovise was at my side. She told me not worry about Jasmine. She said, "You know how much women love your husband."

She can be sympathetic when she wants to be.

I told her, "That's not the part that bothers me. I know my husband is fine, wealthy, and successful. But, do you have to disrespect me? Can you flirt when I am not around?"

I know Jasmine does not like me. I approached my husband about her. Needless to say, I never like his responses. He says I don't have anything to worry about. Her actions say otherwise. Jasmine was driving a wedge between us.

Jasmine's boyfriend was murdered. Jaime's father represented Paul when he was alive. When he died, his family claimed everything leaving Jasmine on the street with nothing. Jaime offered her a job and a place to stay. He paid the first month's rent, then his father paid it until she was able to pay. She has fucked everybody in the kitchen and now she's working her way through management.

Altovise and I sat down to finish lunch. Stephan joined us while Jaime took care of management business.

We had a few laughs. Stephan ate some crab cake and sipped some wine. Altovise told him about the trip to the Poconos.

Stephan said, "Girl, you already know I cannot go on no trips until summer. I don't like snow."

Jaime finally returned to the table. Altovise and I said nothing. Jaime sipped his wine and talked. When we didn't say anything, Jaime asked, "Not talking to me?"

♥

When we got in that fancy Mercedes Benz, I let his black ass have it.

"You need to fire that bitch!"

Jaime pounded his hands on the steering wheel.

"What the hell, Shanti?" he asked, "what's the problem now? She is a great manager."

I yelled so loud at him that I scared my own damn self.

"Really? All of your employees that's been there since you opened do nothing but complain about this girl. Nobody says anything good about her. In fact, they say she sashays around the restaurant like she owns the place, throws fits when she does not get her way, and complains. Why is she there?" I asked.

Jaime said nothing. I went in the condo and went to bed without saying goodnight to him. He fell asleep on the couch in the living room. The next day I showered, dressed, ate breakfast, and went to work without saying a word to Jaime.

♥

It was a slow day at work. I was preoccupied with the argument I had with Jaime the night before. Even when Brendan brought in treats for us, it didn't make me feel better.

"Yo, have you seen Lupe?" Brendan asked as he walked towards Gisselle and I with a bag of Burger King, a tray of Starbucks drinks, and a box of Krispy Kreme donuts.

Gisselle and I laughed. Here his ass comes with all this food and he's talking about Lupe. I leaned on the host podium. Brendan is about six-foot-three with a slim build and he's funny as hell. He's a clown. He's another one of Jaime's frat brothers. Brendan works at the Annapolis and Harbor locations.

"You talking about Lupe but you got Burger King, Starbucks, and Krispy Kreme?" I asked. Brendan placed the goodies on the bar.

"Yo, I got fifty-five orders on my way in."

"You didn't ask me if I wanted anything," I said as he handed over a tall vanilla bean frappe with extra whip and caramel. "Thanks," I responded.

Brendan is my work husband. He calls the restaurant or my cell phone and asks if I would like something to eat or drink. I could have fifty cups of coffee and I'll ask for the fifty-first cup from Brendan. He doesn't take any money. He will bring lunch, snacks, and leftovers from home.

"I'm going upstairs to check on the new girls," Gisselle said as she took her pen and clipboard and left.

Brendan stood next to me and straightened his tie. I shrugged. He looked nice. He's always so polished and put together.

"New girls?" Brendan asked with a frown as he pulled up a stool from the bar and sat next to me. "I thought Jaime said he wasn't hiring anybody else?"

I sipped my drink, not really caring what my husband did. I could not shake the funk I was in. I was deeply concerned about Jaime and there was no one I could talk to.

"Yo, what is wrong with Jasmine?" Brendan asked.

I turned to him.

He continued, "Shanti, she came in yesterday at about 4:00 p.m. She was supposed to come in at 12:00 p.m. for her shift. Jasmine got on my damn nerves. I sent her home. She called Jaime."

I asked, "What did Jaime say?"

"This fool. Oh my God, Ashanti. You cannot go against your brother for that piece of ass. She fucking Damien."

I pulled my straw away from my mouth. "Cecil's son?"

"Yes."

Brendan stood as a party of four walked in.

"Be back, Shanti."

"Okay, Love."

He grabbed four menus from the side of the podium, then turned to the party and escorted them upstairs.

Brendan was my relief. Once he ate lunch and got situated, I left and went to my office to see what was going on. I had a decent clientele and reputation. Sherri was falling behind with clients.

She called me the night before and said, "Sis, you got to come in and help."

Gisselle called while I was at the office. I texted Brendan and asked him what was going on? He apologized and said he didn't know that Gisselle was calling me. I told him whatever was going on, ask her and take care of it. Jaime is not paying him six figures for nothing.

I had closed on a multimillion-dollar home in Towson. I was going to give the couple the keys. I was headed up Charles Street on my way to Towson. I told the couple that I had been working with for over six months I was on the way. Gisselle called once more. I was so frustrated. It had to have been an emergency. I usually don't answer, but something told me to answer this time.

Gisselle said that Jasmine wasn't at work. I asked her where Brendan was. She said that he was in the office on the phone with the door closed talking to Chance. Chance and Jaime met in college. He's older than Jaime and the overseer at Annapolis.

Gisselle said she tried to tell Brendan numerous times but a rush of customers had come into the restaurant. On top of the lunch rush, there was also a party of twenty that was on the reservations for the day. Gisselle said that they were on a two-hour wait and the kitchen was backed up. See, this is why Gisselle got the assistant manager/trainer position. She's prompt. Jasmine was supposed to be at work at 9:00 a.m. It was going on 12:00 p.m. Once again, she was a no call no show. She has done this numerous times. Van has corrected her. He has even written her up. Van does not play with her. Stephan lets her know every time she fucks up that she is a fuck up. He's said on numerous occasions that he does not understand why she has a job.

I told Gisselle that I would call Jaime once I finished with my clients. I hung up with her to call Belle and let her know what was going on.

"Belle, I'm in the middle of money, can you handle this?"

Belle said, "I get off at 2:00 p.m. There is no mid shift manager."

"Is Jaime there?" I asked my dear aunt.

She wouldn't lie to me. She said that Jaime was with Chris, Brendan, Chase, and Juan in a meeting over in the Gallery. So, they weren't at work and had no idea what was going on. I am sure Jaime got a message or a text.

By the time Belle and I got off the phone, another employee told her that Jasmine was in the emergency room.

I wasn't feeling well at all. After I finished up with my clients, I went home. As soon as I walked in the door, I let Jaime have it. I told him I was tired of his staff calling me about Jasmine. I told him that she's a problem and she needs to be dealt with. He said he did not have time for my shit and told me to shut the fuck up.

I reminded him that we worked too hard to let some skank come in and destroy what we'd built together. He said nothing. I had nothing else to say. I went to bed without dinner.

♥

"Oh, oh, oh, it's The Tom Joyner Morning Show," Sherri sang throughout the office.

My sister puts me in a good mood. I don't care what kind of a rotten mood I am in, she knows what to do and say to make it better.

Sherri sat across from me. I was on the other side of the round table trying to drink some hot chai tea. It was not working. I was nauseated. It was not a good morning and it was raining.

Sherri was in the middle of filing when she sat down to take a small break. She's so pretty, round, and brown with a lot of damn hair. I don't know where all that hair came from. When we were growing up, she had the least amount of hair. Sherri exhaled loudly. I looked up from the cup of hot chai tea and snickered.

"Something wrong?" she asked.

I lowered my eyes.

She shrugged as she grabbed a pile of files from the middle of the table.

"You don't have to tell me, I can call Altovise," she said.

There was a long pause. I shook my head. I wasn't in the mood to talk but being with her made me feel better.

"Or…," she said as she stood to her feet and placed the files under her arm, "I can call Jaime."

I shrugged. "Jaime is cheating on me."

Sherri dropped the files on the table. I am sure she did not mean to. I helped her pick up the files and made sure all the proper papers went into the right folders.

"What?" she was genuinely surprised.

"Don't act so surprised," I said as I handed her the last file.

She took it and placed the pile on the table. Sherri held her mouth with both of her hands. I sat back down and crossed my legs.

"When did you find out?" Sherri whispered as if we were in a room full of people when it was just the two of us.

Sherri came in for a hug. I hugged her back.

"Last night," I said while tears welled up in my eyes. "And on top of that, I think I am pregnant."

Sherri backed up and shook her head. I could see that she was disgusted, surprised, and confused.

There was a knock at the door and Sherri went to answer it. We weren't expecting anyone. I grabbed my lukewarm cup of chai tea and walked over to the sink on the other side of the room. I poured the drink down the drain. Sherri came back to the sink with a dozen roses and a couple boxes from Shari's Berries.

"Look at this," she said as she smiled like a kid at Christmas.

She had already opened the note that came with the beautiful long-stemmed rose arrangement.

"I am sorry about last night. Will you forgive me? Love, Jaime."

Sherri shook her head. She was suckered in. This is what my husband does. He does shit that gets under my skin or he mistreats me, then he tries to buy me back. I took the arrangement from Sherri and told her she could have the berries. She was overjoyed.

"Have a caramel pretzel. I forgive him," she said while opening the box and handing over a pretzel.

I took one bite of the pretzel and instantly felt nauseous; it did not sit right in my stomach. I leaned over the sink and threw up. *I cannot be pregnant. Not now*, I thought to myself. I had always dreamed of having a baby with Jaime. I always wondered what he or she would look like. We weren't trying for a baby, but we were making love every night and morning before work. We didn't use protection and I wasn't on birth control, so it was only a matter of time before I got pregnant.

I'll never forget when I finally decided to go on a diet and tried to shed some pounds. I work a few blocks over from Lexington Market. Every morning I had a hot dog smothered in sauerkraut, chili, and cheese. I ate pancakes, grits, home fries, and sausages. I had a donut in one hand, turkey leg in the other, and a baked potato sitting in front of me. Sherri asked was I pregnant. I said, no. She smiled and said ok.

Jaime and I decided to head down to Virginia Beach for some rest and relaxation. The morning of our trip, I woke up, then threw up. Jaime asked was I okay. I said yes. I told him that I ate way too much at work.

He said, "Be careful eating that greasy food, it will repeat on you. It's good but not all the time."

I had breast augmentation surgery a month prior to the vacation. I had fat transferred from my hips and thighs and injected into my breasts. It was a gift from my husband. I always wanted a lift. I didn't want silicone. We did research and I headed down to Miami to have the procedure done.

I recovered in Lionel's condo on Miami Beach. He lives in Scarsdale, New York, but comes down to Miami in the winter with his family. He's also a personal chef for football players and rappers down there. The condo has a waitstaff of five. There was always someone on duty. I was there healing for three months. The driver was the only one that lived on the premises along with the head maid. She was sweet. I was waited on hand and foot. I woke up to breakfast every day. And if I wanted anything, all I had to do was ask.

I had a driver take me anywhere I wanted to go. The beach was outside of my bedroom window. I had a picture-perfect view of the ocean. It was literally feet away. The sound of the ocean was so soothing.

While I was down in Miami, I did some shopping. I needed some new clothes and bras to go with my new body. But I was lonely. I missed my family. Jaime came down on the weekends and spent as much time with me as he could. He was just about to open Towson Pete's. The grand opening was weeks away.

He said, "Baby, you have to get better."

I agreed. I was ready to go. There is nothing like a getaway, but I was missing Baltimore and it seemed like everyone I ran into was from Maryland.

When my breasts began to hurt, I attributed it to the surgery and the fact that Jaime could not keep his hands off me.

"You ready?" he asked

I nodded as I grabbed my Versace sunglasses. The car was packed, gassed up, and ready to go.

"Wait," I said.

I had to use the bathroom. It felt like I had to poop. I sat down on the cold seat and buckled over. I felt something slide out of my vagina. Shit, I got my period. I got my washcloth and wiped then I screamed for Jaime. My heart raced. I broke out in a cold sweat. There was a clump of blood in my hand.

Jaime pushed the door open. I stood up and blood ran down my legs. It looked like a murder scene. I slowly turned and looked down. There was a baby in the toilet. I pointed. Jaime moved in closer. He looked in, scooped up the fetus, and looked at me in disbelief.

"I had no clue, Baby," I said.

Jaime backed up into the corner. He did not want to let the baby go. I lost my husband that night. He hasn't been the same since I had my miscarriage. I thought it was going to bring us closer, instead it tore us apart.

I don't know what to do. I am at a loss. I feel like I am in this alone. I try to keep a brave face. And now, what if I am pregnant again? I don't want to do this again. I can't go through another heartbreak. What will happen if I am pregnant again?

Chapter Six

LONELY HEART

I excused myself from the table to see what was going on. I didn't like the vibe in the restaurant. Something happened and I was determined to get to the bottom of it. Between the sounds of the pans crashing and laughter coming from the kitchen, my wife and Altovise together are horrible, and all I want is peace and quiet. I wanted to spend the afternoon with my wife. I don't need an audience. I should've taken her home and cooked for her like I started to.

As soon as I sat down at my desk and turned on the MacBook, there was a knock at the door. I exhaled. It did not sound like a friendly, "Hey, how are you, Jaime?" type of knock.

I braced myself for whatever was on the other side of the door.

"Yeah." I leaned back in the chair and prayed it was all good.

"Got a minute?" Belle stuck her head in the door. I exhaled and offered her the chair in front of me. She came inside and shut the door lightly.

"What is going on in here?" she asked as she sat down. "I am tired of every time I come to work there is an issue with Jasmine."

"What now?" I asked.

I was frustrated with Jasmine. I knew it would be wrong to fire her with all that was going on in her life, but I know she's got a thing for me and I don't see her in that way. She's slept with every man in the kitchen. They passed her around like a blunt. Nobody wants to wife her. I heard she gives good head but that's not enough to tear me away from my wife.

Jasmine is smart and she's a beautiful girl. I want to help her because no one else will. She burned bridges and alienated her family for Paul. Paul's family thinks she got him murdered. I had my suspicions. She was fucking a guy behind Paul's back. Supposedly Paul got another chick pregnant and she sought revenge. Turns out that was a lie and the other female wasn't pregnant at all. The night Paul was murdered, they were coming from the comedy club in Columbia. Some dudes ran up on him and killed him. Jasmine didn't get injured or even grazed in the hail of bullets. He was shot more than twenty-one times with three different guns.

"She keeps calling out. She tried it today, but I told her she couldn't. So, now she's in the bathroom throwing up. We don't need this drama, Jaime. This is the third time this week and it's only Tuesday. Do you want me to decrease her hours or what?"

Belle does all of the scheduling. She eventually sat down with me and told me it was becoming too much, so I hired a human resources team and they are doing a good job. Then, I hired Brendan's wife, Mila, to run the marketing and promotions team that's taking Pete's to another level. Mila used to work for corporate America. She knows the ins and outs of running a business. She left her six-figure corporate job to work for us. I can match her pay, but I am going to wait on that.

"Let me deal with that. What's the special for today?" I asked, changing the subject.

"Oven fried chicken breast with mashed potatoes, side salad, green beans with potatoes, and ham," Belle answered.

"Damn." Belle and I laughed together. "Make me a plate and send it over to the table where Ashanti is."

"Okay," she said as she walked out the door.

Her mood had definitely changed from when she walked in, let me tell you.

"Thanks," I said as picked up the phone and dialed Jasmine's cell phone. I know this girls number by heart.

She answered on the second ring, "Hello."

"Jasmine."

"Yeah."

"What's wrong?"

"I'm sick."

"You been sick for a while. Do you need to go to the doctor?"

"I'm pregnant."

"By who?" That was a million-dollar question with a two-million-dollar answer and the chance of a heart attack upon finding out the answer.

God knows I don't like to pry. I should've kept it at, "Do you need to go to the doctor?" But I opened my big ass mouth and called Red in the office.

"Yo."

He was covered in flour from head to toe. Red is my right hand. I can't do anything without him, and vice versa. Terrence Howard should've been his father instead of my black ass Uncle Rick.

"Jasmine's pregnant."

Red laughed. "Shut the fuck up."

He sat down in the chair across from me, crossed his legs, and pulled a cigarette from behind his ear.

"Who's the father?" he asked as he lit up.

"You, Nigga," I said as I stood to my feet.

Red dropped his cigarette and pulled a fat blunt from his other ear.

He shook his head and said, "You can't get pregnant out your ass son."

My eyes widened.

"She in the bathroom throwing up?" Red asked.

I nodded as I leaned back in the chair and rocked.

"So, it is true. You fucked her in my walk in?" I asked.

"Dude, she sucked this dick in the walk in. I took her ass over to the hotel and slut her ass out. I didn't nut in that bitch. I fucked her in the ass with two condoms."

We laughed. Red held out his hand. We slapped fives.

"I don't trust her. I didn't even stay the night. She was all over me, so I said fine. She had her period. I told her I don't do that shit," Red added.

"Nigga, since when?" I asked as I folded my arms across my chest. "You ran red lights in college and high school."

"Damn. Jasmine better find her baby daddy cause it ain't me. I wore condoms that night, Kid."

"Okay, she in some shit. I don't even know if she's really pregnant or not," I exhaled.

"Well, if she is, I feel sorry for her," Red added.

"I have to see what's going on," I said.

"Cool. We done? I wanna go smoke this blunt," Red said as he got up and walked towards the door.

"Yeah."

I dismissed Red and watched as he walked out the door. I was overwhelmed with sadness. Hearing the heartbreak in Jasmine's voice when she told me she was pregnant broke my heart. And to listen to my cousin say how sorry he felt for Jasmine made me feel worse. I leaned back in my chair and closed my eyes. I felt bad for Jasmine. I would love for her to meet someone and fall in love like I had with Ashanti.

♥

Do I remember the happy times Ashanti and I shared? Were there ever happy times? Can I recall those happy times like a picture? Of course, I can. I wouldn't have married her if we did not have happy times. Yes, we had our ups and downs and we fought. But to tell you the honest truth, as quiet as is kept, I would do it all over again. We shared the best part of our lives together. I will admit that I was not a good husband. I provided for her financially and I was always there for her sexually, but I wasn't there mentally. That is the most important part of a marriage--communication. I didn't appreciate her when I had her. It was always about the business. When I opened Pete's, I lost my marriage. I lost my wife. I almost lost my damn mind too.

Seeing my mother at her lake house was always refreshing. I called her and told her I'd be down alone for the weekend just to think. There is no cell phone reception at the lake house. Ashanti and I had gone together a couple of months ago. We had a good time, just the two of us.

She loves the mall that's about five miles from the lake. There is a gym across the street from the lake, so I took her to get a pedicure and spa treatment, then I took her to do a little shopping. When we were done, we had lunch at this vegan restaurant. I was still hungry, so we went home and fired up the grill. Ashanti decided to take a nap. She asked me to wake her when dinner was ready. I made ribs, corn, baked beans, and potato salad. I even invited Luke, Samantha, and their kids from across the lake over to join us.

I checked on Ashanti. She looked so peaceful sleeping that I did not want to wake her. I kissed her forehead and rejoined our neighbors from across the lake. We ate, sipped whiskey, and smoked cigars while watching the kids on their jet skis and parasails.

Ashanti finally joined us after her nap. It was getting late and Samantha was tired and ready to go to bed. They retired to the sailboat and sailed across the lake. Ashanti sat on my lap and before long she was asleep again. The next morning, I made omelets, then we left for the city. Back to work. Back to the hustle. Back to the grind. Back to, "Team, let's get this money."

I needed a place to escape to. I was so glad Mama was not at the lake house. I went alone, but I told Ashanti I was going to visit my mother. It's never a good idea when the two of them are around one another. The claws come out. It's super ugly.

♥

I returned home from the lake house on Sunday morning. Ashanti dropped me off at work and went back home to rest. I made it just in time for the Sunday Brunch. We open at eleven for brunch. I am always at the front of the house, expediting. If it gets busy, I run food. There is a fifty percent chance I'll be running food during brunch. There are two seatings: 11:00 a.m. until 12:30 p.m. and 1:00 p.m. until 2:30 p.m. We close at 2:30 p.m. and re-open at 4:00 p.m. for dinner service. I stay all day on Sundays. I don't see my wife, my family, or my friends. I am at the restaurant from 8:00 in the morning until 11:00 at night. On Monday's, I travel from restaurant to restaurant to see how everything is going. That will take me until 5:00 p.m., then I go home and rest until it is time to do it all over again.

Chapter Seven

•>>>>>>>•<<<<<<<•

THE GOOD WIFE

Jaime and I have been married for ten beautiful years. We've been together for twenty. We met through a mutual girlfriend, Sanaa Miller. Rumor was Sanaa had a thing for me. I couldn't tell. My head was so far in the clouds; I was head over heels in love with Jaime. He was the only man on my mind.

Sanaa and Altovise were the best of friends. I don't know how they got along. They are total opposites. Mama said they balanced each other out. Sanaa used to come to every party Altovise promoted. Even the house parties Altovise threw while Mama and Pops were away with church retreats and getaways. Sanaa was there and she was always fly. She outdressed everybody, even Altovise.

Altovise threw the bomb parties. Anybody who was anybody was there. Jaime said the reason Altovise's parties were so popular was because of him.

I said, "Nah, Shorty, my sister was way popular before we even met you."

Altovise said she knew Jaime from campus. Jaime went to Morgan State University. He played football for about three semesters. During his senior year, he broke his leg and put the football dream to the side. His mother was hot. Jaime could've recovered easily from his injury, but he knew his heart was in the kitchen.

Altovise threw a Valentine's Day concert and after party for local artists. It was the hottest party in Baltimore. The party spilled over to Mama's house. It was 3:00 in the morning. Mama and Pops were on another getaway for the church. Mama is a deaconess and Pops is on the usher board, but he was always in tow with Mama on trips. I was in the bed knocked out when all of a sudden there was a knock on my bedroom door that startled me out of my sleep. My heart sank. Who was knocking on my bedroom door that hard in the middle of the night? I almost pissed my pants. I was afraid to get up and see who it was. Then I heard a female voice say, "My bad." She laughed. I assumed she thought it was the bathroom. I couldn't go back to sleep. There was too much excitement going on downstairs. I got out of bed and went to investigate.

The living room, dining room, and kitchen was full of people. They had all kinds of alcohol and food. Jaime was there. He fired up the stove and made brown sugar pecan and banana waffles. There was a line of people forming to get in the kitchen to get those buttermilk, sweet, sugary, . and sticky waffles. I pushed past everybody and shook my head when I saw him cooking and serving everyone.

"Hey, Baby, want a plate?" I lowered my head in my chest and laughed. It was bananas how everyone responded to his food. People were licking the paper plates. Somebody asked if he was cooking lunch. No, you gots to get up out of here.

♥

When I first began my business, Mama and Daddy were against it. Daddy said I should invest my money into something like a hair salon or a flower shop. I didn't want to do that.

Then Mama said, "It's not what you know, it's who you know."

I knew I was going to be good at real estate. Being Jaime Harris' wife opened doors I thought would be impossible to open. When God says yes, no man, woman, or child can say no.

It just so happens that I was with Jaime when Dannon Hill came into the restaurant. It was Dannon's first time at Pete's. And of course, being the huge football star that Dannon is, Jaime was immediately notified. All of his friends and celebrity friends eat for free. I was coming out of the walk in. I had on a black knee-length skirt; red bottoms; matching diamond tennis bracelet, earrings, and necklace; and my hair was pulled back into a tight, sleek ponytail. My face was beat. Jaime called me over to the table. I straightened my skirt as I made my way to the table that sat five really big football players. I was a little intimidated.

When I reached the table and stood by Jaime, all talk stopped, and all eyes fell upon my flesh. Uh oh. I smiled and shook each hand while firmly looking each one of the guys in their eyes. Then, I stood back and crossed my arms. Jaime wrapped his left arm around me and told the table that I was his beautiful wife and that I have a real estate business.

One of the players put his beer down and asked, "Do you have a card? I need somewhere to stay for the season."

"Are you renting, or do you want to own?" I responded.

"I'm looking to own," he said. "My wife is from here and my kids go to school here. I travel a lot."

Every meeting with a friend of Jaime's always turns into a business venture of some sort. You constantly have to be on your game with him, so I always have business cards ready. I keep a Tiffany & Co. business card case in my pocket with at least five cards in it. Every day before I leave the house, I make sure it is on me. And when I return home, if I have one card left, I did good. If I have none, mission accomplished. If I don't give out any or the person who said they were going to call doesn't, it's okay. I don't beat myself up.

My initial meeting with Dannon took place at my office. I've had this office building for going on five years now. I decided to step out on my own after a long talk with my husband. I worked for an independent real estate firm for about six months. It didn't go the way I planned. Jaime said to look for a building and we would go from there.

I invited Dannon to my office. His wife and mother-in-law tagged along. I had coffee, chai tea, bagels, cream cheese, donuts, and a fruit and cheese platter ready. His wife was impressed. She was the tallest piece of chocolate. Gorgeous with long legs, dimples, a short fade haircut, and popping lip gloss. She sat down, crossed her legs, and looked around the office shaking her head in approval.

Once the meeting was over, she told Dannon and her mom to go on. She said she wanted to speak to me. We walked over to the reception desk.

She said, "Ashanti, I am so impressed. I was so happy when I walked through those doors and saw another sister."

We laughed.

"Some of Dannon's friend's wives don't look like you and I," she giggled. "I'm so happy."

I nodded.

She went on, "I have a couple girlfriends that are interested in purchasing property. Do you mind if I give them your card?"

"Not at all."

"Great. I'll be in touch."

She gave me a hug and a kiss on the cheek, then she left. Her fragrance lingered in the office for hours. Elliott asked what I was wearing. I told him that was Dannon's wife's perfume.

About a month later, the leaves were turning orange, the sun was setting a little early, and it was time to pull those sweaters out of the closet. My favorite time of the year, fall, was upon us. And soon after that Halloween, and you know the rest. I was sitting in the office at Pete's sipping on some hot apple cider and snacking on a huge slice of pecan pie fresh from the bakery when the phone rang.

"Pete's."

"Ashanti?" It was Plenean Carter, Dannon's wife. She kept her maiden name.

"Yes." I sat up in the chair and pushed my pie to the side.

"I have one of my girlfriends on the line. She just lost her job at a hair salon. She's looking to open her own. Can you help her?"

"Sure."

I could not wait to get home and tell Jaime what happened. We were so busy at the restaurant that I didn't have a chance to call him to tell him my good news of having another potential client.

"Look at you."

Jaime and I had asparagus, crab cakes, filet mignon, and seafood risotto for dinner that night. He lit candles and light jazz music was playing. It was really romantic.

"I am so proud of you," Jaime said as he sat a flute of champagne down on the table.

"Thank you, Baby," I said as he placed a strawberry in the flute. I sipped. "Guess who called me earlier today at work?"

Jaime shrugged as he focused on the food.

"It was Plenean Carter, Dannon Hill's wife. She called with Mia Alexander on the line."

"Get out of here. What happened to ABC?" Jaime asked as he took the crab cakes from the broiler. They were the size of baseballs.

I shrugged, "She said Misha spent the money."

Misha was the owner and senior cosmetologist at Another Bad Creation salon in downtown Baltimore around the corner from the famous Lexington Market. Man, that place brings back so many memories. My mama used to take me there every Saturday morning. Misha did my mother's hair and Mia's uncle, Wes, did my hair.

I was sixteen when I met Mia Alexander. She was the new "it girl." When Mia left ABC, it went down. Tracey, Misha's sister, took over and ran the place into the ground. She was stealing money. She wasn't buying products or paying bills. Misha started snorting dope with Wes.

Mama said, "Don't nobody convince you to snort dope."

She said that Misha was always snorting dope, she just found someone to do it with. Wes put away coke like a vacuum cleaner. I used to see him taking lines. I even saw him doing lines at the shampoo bowl.

Wes was always high when he came to work. He's what they call a functioning addict. He was a bad ass stylist. He used to travel between Baltimore and Atlanta doing hair. He cleared $5,000.00 a week and smoked it all up. Sad. Such a beautiful, talented soul gone to waste.

"I'm proud of you, Baby," Jaime said, "Keep up the good work. Don't slack off. Our busy time of the year at Pete's is coming up. I'm going to need you there as well."

I smiled and replied, "I won't let you down, Love."

Between October and February, Pete's is slammed. Mama is even busy during this time of year. Mama called Jaime and asked him did we have a couple people to work some shifts? We couldn't loan any people out. I wish I could help Mama, but I have to work at Pete's.

Jaime and I used to work with Mama, but ever since Pete's took off, we can't.

We are always looking for holiday help. It's overwhelming. There was this one young lady that came into the restaurant and stole my heart. Her name is Betty Reyes. We call her Church Betty, but there is nothing churchy about her. Betty is a little rough around the edges. She can get ratchet and hood. That's why we love her. She's real. I believe that with a little guidance, she will turn out just fine.

Betty came into the bakery and took over. Marcia, the bakery manager, was able to take a day off and relax. It's something Marcia hasn't been able to do in a while. We're grateful for Betty. I don't know where we would be without her.

On top of running the restaurant and the real estate business, I also helped Jaime set up an online bakery.

We had to move into another condo because we ran out of space. He remodeled the kitchen with baking stoves. Now, it looks like a bakery.

I walked into the office and Aunt Belle and Jaime were sitting at the desk listening to Pandora. "Hey, two of my favorite people."

Belle smiled as she stood up, "Hey, Honey, how are you?"

"I'm a little tired but I'm okay," I smiled as Jaime winked. "So, I have some orders that came in while you two were having a meeting."

Jaime took the paper from my hands and exhaled.

"What's wrong, Baby?" I asked.

"It's becoming too much," Belle added.

"There is a space over in the Gallery Mall, it's about half of the rent I am paying here," Jaime said as he exhaled, leaned back in the chair and, rocked. "I can hire a couple people to help out."

I sat down and exhaled too. In the midst of my business ventures, I was neglecting my husband and I felt bad.

"Can you excuse us, Aunt Belle?" I asked.

I waited until the door was closed.

"Why didn't you tell me?" I asked Jaime.

"Ashanti, you got all your stuff going on. I didn't want to tell you."

"But, Baby, we are in this together. I can't let this business suffer."

"You can't let your business suffer. We can't do both."

"Okay, so Sherri and Elliott can officially take over?"

"Ashanti, listen, this is my dream. Harris and Harris is your dream. I don't want you to take on more responsibility. I'm going to hire some more people."

"Can we afford it?" I asked.

Jaime turned to the printer, pulled a piece of paper out of the slot, and handed it to me. I looked over the numbers.

"And if I want, I can toss another Pete's in," Jaime bragged.

My eyes widened when I saw the numbers for the quarter. I looked up at him. Jaime nodded. "Wow," I said as I sunk into the chair.

"Towson is doing good and Van's over at Annapolis is doing absolutely wonderful. I'll hire a dream team and let them take over. I don't want our dreams to die."

"Wow, Baby."

"So, if you don't mind. Can you put the word out for me, hire some good people to run the marketing department, get an accountant, payroll, and all of that? We are getting so big that we can't do it all."

"Yes, Love."

Jaime's phone buzzed. I looked over at it. He picked it up and placed it face down.

"Who was that?"

"Some friends from college are in town," he giggled nervously.

"Oh, okay, are you meeting up or something?"

"Maybe. Look, I have to get to work and so do you."

I stood up, "Yes, Love. I'll get on it."

It was getting closer to the holiday. Jaime had a huge staff holiday meeting with all restaurants at the Harbor location. I don't think we will ever have one of those ever again. We closed all locations at 7:00 on Sunday evening, met up at the Harbor around 9:00 p.m., and the meeting went well into the midnight hour. We went over the Thanksgiving bake sale, the pre-Thanksgiving bake sale, and our Halloween party.

Jaime and I kicked off our first annual Pete's family Halloween costume ball for kids. We decorated the restaurant in creepy Halloween decorations. The staff dressed up in costumes. We had candy, giveaways for the best costumes, hot dogs, cheeseburgers, hamburgers with red and green relish, and fries in the shape of creepy kitty cats and ghosts. There was also a salad bar for the adults. Everyone had a good time, we had tons and tons of candy.

Jaime was overwhelmed with the success of his restaurant. He started going out more and coming to work less. I had no choice but to stop working at the firm in order to work at the restaurant. Every morning I would ask my husband was he coming in. Nope. I was worried. I was beginning to think it was too much. On top of it all, the holidays were approaching, and he was in talks about opening another Pete's. I wanted him to slow down, but the restaurant's his dream.

"Hello," Monica said as she walked into the office.

She did not look happy. I put the phone down.

"What's wrong?" I asked.

"Rachael and Pamela Jackson are sitting at the bar."

I exhaled. "So, that's the college friend that's in town."

"Yeah and she asked Nick the bartender for Jaime's phone number. I overheard Nick telling Gisselle."

Rachael and Jaime were lovers. Pam is her flunky. Pam is everybody's flunky. I hate that stank ass bitch. She is pure evil. I don't know what her problem is with me, but she needs to correct it. I refused to go and see what was going on. I don't like confrontations. They are so bold that they will try it with me. I stayed in the office with Monica for the duration of my shift. I have to talk to Jaime about this.

Chapter Eight

REMINISCE

I have a serious problem with Rachael and her click. Mama said they're jealous of Jaime and me. But this happened way before Jaime and me. This stuff with Jaime and I is just the icing on the cake. They had their chances with Jaime. Back in the day, Rachael, Arica, Sloan, Claudia, and Jordan were best friends. I think they are jealous of one another. Rachael and Jordan were tight in college; inseparable. Claudia and I were close growing up. I never hung around Rachael. I am the youngest out of the bunch. Claudia and I are closer in age. Claudia was something like my best friend.

I only know of Rachael because of Jaime. I don't know her personally. I've never sat in the same room with her or even spoken to her. Claudia never spoke about Rachael to me because I had no interest in doing drugs, smoking weed, or drinking. They were having sex and going on dates while I was in the house watching *Full House* and *Family Matters*.

Arica, Sloan, and Jordan used to get their hair done at ABC. They had jobs that required them to work Saturday mornings, but when they did occasionally come in on a Saturday, they were timid. They never said anything or tried anything with me because Mia would've fought them, straight up.

When Another Bad Creation salon closed, they took the drama to Sittin' Pretty owned by this smut bucket, Erica. Erica and her pig nosed ass sister, Sophia, are troublemakers. They are into more shit than doing hair. They were the ones that started the rumor about Misha doing drugs, saying that she must've gotten the bug cause she's so thin. I never paid those rumors any mind.

♥

When ABC salon closed, Mia began working at Sittin' Pretty Salon. She has too much class to work at Sittin' Pretty though. I even told Mia that. I never stepped foot in Sittin' Pretty because those chicks don't like me. Altovise knows them all well. It's funny, they didn't like me, but they took shit from Altovise. Nobody wanted smoke with Altovise.

Altovise, Jordan, and Chuck's ex-wife, Karen, were good friends. They were super tight. You would've thought they were sisters. Karen is not like them. Karen is quiet, she keeps to herself, and isn't into drama.

After Karen had Monica, she got her GED and enrolled in college. She studied hard, worked three jobs, and when she had enough credits, she enrolled at Howard. I was proud of Karen.

Altovise used to go to Howard University's home-coming with Karen. Altovise would get a hotel room and have parties.

Altovise's so-called fake ass best friend, She-She, came with Karen to one of Altovise's hotel parties. She-She never mentioned to Altovise that she knew Karen. Why not, I don't know.

When she saw Altovise at the party, She-She said, "Oh, I didn't know you knew Karen like that." She-She was shady and loved to cause trouble.

Altovise said, "Karen lived with me and my family when she was pregnant with Monica." She-She asked Altovise did she know that Karen was dating Chuck. Altovise, being the snake that she is, said that she didn't know Karen's baby daddy but she heard that he was married. Karen hid Chuck from us until the divorce. Shortly after the divorce, he married Karen, and they had Monica.

She-She knows Chuck's first wife. She-She told Altovise that Chuck's first wife said he may be a fat ass but he took care of her sexual needs. They had a good laugh about it. Meanwhile, my sister was scheming.

Altovise finagled her way into Chuck and Karen's marriage. Monica had to have been about six or seven. All I remember was Karen crying to Claudia about Chuck cheating on her. Now, who would want Chuck's round ass but Karen?

Jaime and I were at Tommy Woo's Chinese Restaurant down at the Harbor and guess who walked in with

Chuck on her arm? After that, I started looking at my sister differently.

Jaime asked Chuck why he was there with Altovise. He said he was showing her some cars and they ended up down there. I never believed that bullshit ass story. Extremely long story short, Altovise slept with Chuck. Chuck divorced Karen. Chuck married Altovise.

Jordan, Claudia, Sloan, and Arica were bridesmaids in the wedding. Claudia told me that Rachael was at the wedding, but she was not in the wedding party. I refused to go and I dared my sister to say anything to me.

I cussed her out the morning of her wedding, then I gave her $100.00 and paid for her spa day. She had the nerve to call Mama and tell her I was acting unreasonable and that I ruined her day. I said good.

I told her, "You are never going to have good luck. You were a bridesmaid in Karen's wedding along with those snakes Jordan, Claudia, Sloan, and Arica, and here you are marrying her leftovers." Karen was heartbroken.

I don't know who's the worst out of the bunch. Sherri swears it's Sloan. She is very attractive and smart and she married into money as well; but, she still gossips, goes out clubbing, and her baby was taken away from her last year. Sloan asked Jaime to write a letter to CPS, so she could get her son back.

I said, "I hope you said no."

Jaime said sheepishly, "I told her I would think about it." Needless to say, Jaime said no. Sloan said that I was the reason.

Jaime and I took a weekend off just to get away. We saw Mia Alexander and her husband, Jordan, at the Hilton on Peachtree.

She said, "I heard Altovise got married."

I said, "Yes, I don't want to talk about it."

Mia exhaled and said, "Neither do I."

Karen grieved her divorce like it was the end of the world.

The last time I saw Arica Clinton was at ABC salon. She was getting her hair done and she told me that she was pregnant by Black. She was sixteen years old and pregnant by ugly ass Black. I'm not going to lie, Black looks like a gorilla, but he was my dude growing up.

Arica is a grandmother now. Four of her daughters, who are all doing well from what I hear, had babies before they left high school. They are doing better than their trifling ass mother.

Arica used to be so classy. I don't know what happened. Her sister married a football player, but she wants to run around with lowlife ass men. Mama said Arica is looking for the same thing her sister was looking for but in the wrong men.

Arica's mother is a paralegal and her father is a teacher. Jordan used to mess with Black. As a matter of fact, Jordan was pregnant by Black first. Arica and Jordan were good friends. They used to sleep in the same dirty ass bed.

Arica had ran away from home to go live with Jordan on Bond Street. There were sixteen people living in that house. Sherri used to go down there to get her hair braided by Cici. She used to always drag me with her.

Ms. Vincent, Jordan's mother, called my mother at the church and asked her did the church have any mattresses? Mama said she knew of a place that would give her a mattress, she just had to go and pick it up by 5:00 that evening. Ms. Vincent asked Mama could she drive her to the place. Mama said sure.

Mama and I were in the church waiting for Ms. Vincent to come. She never showed up, so we left.

When we drove past the house to see what was going on, Ms. Vincent came to the door and said, "Oh, I thought you were going to bring it."

Mama pulled off. The nerve of her. Altovise said they had rats, mice, roaches, and bed bugs. Arica used to have bed bug bites all over her back, trying to tell people they were freckles.

I was tired of trying to be friends with those girls. I did everything in my power to love them. They never showed me any love or respect. I was surprised at Claudia. She hurt my feelings when I found out that she hit on Jaime. I did not want to believe that she would deceive me by flirting with him. Claudia knew that I was madly in love with Jaime. She asked me, "Are you sure he feels the same way about you?" Why would she ask me that?

Jaime even called me up the day before our wedding and said, "Claudia hit on me."

Claudia was supposed to be in my wedding. I called her when I got off the phone with Jaime and told her never mind. She hasn't spoken to me since and I don't care. Mama said I should've been a bigger person. No, I was tired of them. Things like that had been going on since we were teenagers.

That was not the first time I had to put Claudia in her place. The first time was when we were at Altovise's Fourth of July barbecue at Chuck's mother's house. Chuck's mother does not like Altovise. In fact, she hates her.

Anyway, we were all in the backyard having a ball. Red showed up with Cecil and Tita. Claudia showed up with her husband. She had moved away and gotten married. No one knows where she went and I still don't think they're married.

She spoke to Jaime, but she didn't speak to me. Then, she bumped into me. The second time she bumped into me, I had to put her drunk ass in her place. I told her if she didn't sit down and behave, I was going to kick her ass. I said it nice. She sat down and left me alone.

She had the nerve to call me the next day and apologize.

I said, "Claudia, there is nothing for you to apologize for."

When she did not get the response she was looking for, she went on a fucking Ashanti smear campaign and talked shit to everybody about me. I called her. I told her that I was not scared of her and I want her to keep her lips off me.

I said, "I am not those project chicks that kiss your ass because you think you know how to do hair, you brag about graduating from college, and you drive that outdated ass Benz. You only hang with them because you can't hang with us."

Those chicks put her on a fucking pedestal. When I say they worship her, they worship her like she walks on water.

I did feel sorry for her when Altovise told me that Pamela caught her husband in bed with Jordan. I do not believe Pamela caught nobody in bed though. I think she was in the bed with them.

Claudia went on to marry Black's cousin, Crunch, and Jordan married Black. Jordan was getting back at Claudia and Black. Black cheated on her and Claudia supposedly fucked her over. How crazy is that? They need prayer.

About two Thanksgivings ago, Arica had the nerve to call and ask me of all people could she and the kids stay with Jaime and I. Jaime and I were on the couch enjoying each other. We'd just had dinner at the church and passed out bags of food and clothes for the homeless. We were tired. Jaime told me not to answer the phone. Why didn't I listen to him?

Arica was on the other line asking me could she stay cause her baby father put her out. First of all, how did she get my number? I told Jaime. He has a big heart, so he said they could stay with us for one week. He said the kids could stay in one room and she could stay in the other.

Jaime and I do not live on a bus line, so he got up and drove to the subway metro station to get them. It was cold and snowing. I didn't want those kids to suffer because of her, and I kind of knew she was playing on that because I love those kids. My mother called me and said she left the kids in the bakery one day while she went on a job interview. Mama said she fed the kids, took them home, washed their dirty clothes, and fed them dinner. She said Arica showed up at her house at 7:00 that night. Mama said if it were not for those kids, she would've cussed her out.

I warmed up some turkey, gravy, mashed potatoes, macaroni and cheese, and sweet potatoes for the kids. When they showed up, they washed their hands and smashed. Those kids ate so fast. They were cold and hungry. And you can tell they had been out in the street all day. I left the kitchen, went in my bedroom, and cried.

I didn't want anything from Arica except for her to get her act together and take care of those kids. They were filthy. I threw away the clothes they had and went to Walmart the next day to get them shoes, socks, and outfits. At night, Arica would put the kids to sleep and sneak out. I didn't say anything. I would check on the kids to make sure they were nice, warm, and their bellies were full. The youngest told me that Arica was pregnant. Jaime was pissed.

Now, we told her one week. They came on Thanksgiving night and the kids were out of school until Monday. Well, that week came and went.

During the day, Arica slept and at night she was gone. She had to go. I did not want to put the kids out, I wanted to take care of them. I took them to the mall and I bought them coats, hats, scarves, and gloves. I even bought them some clothes, food, and toys.

Jaime and I argued constantly. He said that it was not my responsibility to take care of her children. I took them to school. I neglected work and focused my attention on taking care of them.

And you know during the holiday we get slammed. Christmas was approaching and this was before Jaime hired the marketing team. I worked from home. Jaime came home and told me they had to go. So, I sat Arica down and told her to smooth it over with her man or whoever she was sneaking out of the house at night to see. She said she couldn't go back because she had gotten into an argument with the mother of the man she was seeing. And you know she messed her family over five times, so she couldn't go stay with them.

I gave her some money. My husband is wealthy. We were not hurting. Arica and I went apartment hunting. She found a cute apartment. Mama helped furnish the place. She was there for about two years. Then, she moved in some man who got her and her sister pregnant at the same time.

Altovise came to the restaurant and said, "Somebody pray. Arica is pregnant by some man, her sister is pregnant by him too, and they got put out the apartment."

I asked Altovise where Arica was staying. Altovise said that her mother took three kids, her other sister took three kids, and Arica had the two-year-old and the newborn. I felt for that girl. Although they talked bad about me and tore me down, I still had love for them.

Chapter Nine

OUR HOLIDAY IN NEW YORK

I would like one holiday without drama. The Thanksgiving after the Arica and the kids fiasco, Jaime wanted to get away. That was one of the best holidays I ever spent with the love of my life. There's no better way to kick off the most beautiful time of the year than in New York.

Jaime showed up at my office with a drop dead gorgeous floral arrangement and two tickets for the 5:00 p.m. train leaving from Penn Station to Grand Central station.

He strolled into the office with a smirk on his face and said, "Come on. I got your bags packed." I smiled as my heart dropped. I love surprises. I didn't waste any time. I locked up the office. I didn't tell my mother and father where I was going. I grabbed my chinchilla hipster Louis Vuitton purse and my Chanel sunglasses and was out.

"Where is the car?" I asked as we stepped out into the snowy Baltimore afternoon.

Downtown Baltimore was especially busy with all of the construction and the heavy holiday traffic. It was a mess and I loved it.

I looked around Charles Street for the car. I couldn't find it. Jaime pointed to the yellow taxicab van, then he took my hand in his and we walked towards it. I could see all of our Louis Vuitton luggage packed in the back.

Jaime opened the back door. I climbed into the warm cab. It felt so good. Once he was settled inside the taxi too, I cuddled up to him, laid my head on his shoulder, and closed my eyes. We had a straight shot to Penn Station; it's only a ten minute drive from my office. But, the holiday traffic was super heavy, it turned into a twenty minute drive. We were moving at a snail's pace. Frustrated drivers were honking their horns in the one lane of traffic headed up Charles. People rushed between the cars to get from one side of the street to the other.

The cab driver finally pulled into the drop off area of Penn Station. He hopped out of the van and grabbed all of our luggage. Jaime reached into his back pocket and pulled out his black leather wallet. It was overflowing with credit cards and cash. He pulled out two twenties and gave it to the gracious driver. I thought that man was going to kiss Jaime. Jaime grabbed his Louis Vuitton duffle and garment bags, and I grabbed my matching Louis Vuitton luggage and my Chanel makeup bag with all my Yves Saint Laurent, Chanel, and MAC makeup inside. I never leave home without my makeup bag and Jaime knows it.

Once Jaime and I checked in, we strolled over to the café. I got a hot chocolate. Jaime got the last bear claw. Once we were settled in and waiting to board the train, I asked him for a bite of his bear claw. He gave me a toe. I sat waiting for him to give me another bite. Nope.

He smiled and said, "I love you."

My husband and I share a lot of things, but sweets are not one of them. Jaime loves sweets. He can't get enough of them.

I could hear the train pull up to the platform. Jaime was on his cell phone talking to his mother. She's so damn nosy. She asked him where we were staying, how long we would be gone, and so on and so on.

I asked Jaime to wake me once the drink cart opened. How about he woke me up once we were in Manhattan. I forgot how cold it is in New York. It was bone chilling. Jaime found a cab. The cab driver jumped out and put all of our luggage into the trunk of the cab. Jaime gave the driver two twenties and he whisked us away to The Plaza hotel.

The last time Jaime and I stayed at The Plaza hotel was for Lionel and Angela's wedding. It was only for two nights but it was the best two nights of my life. I felt like royalty. Those rooms are not cheap. They are really something nice for a girl like me coming from where I'm from. Never in a million years would I imagine staying in a hotel were royalty stays. It's absolutely breathtaking. There is no way Jaime planned this getaway on a whim. This took serious planning. It was the holiday and I am sure it was hard to get in. He had to have planned it months in advance. Maybe a year, who knows.

As soon as we got to the room, I unpacked. Check in was at 3:00 p.m. We arrived a little after 8:00 p.m. The staff was so accommodating. We were gifted with a cheese and fruit platter, champagne, and crystal flutes. The room looked like someone's house.

Jaime said we were only staying for a couple of days, but he packed enough lingerie for me for a week.

"You did good, Love," I told him.

Jaime was up at dawn. He ordered breakfast while I slept. I woke to fresh orange juice in tall flutes, bacon, eggs, croissants, pastries, tea, and a bottle of champagne with strawberries. There was a knock at the door. Jaime jumped up to answer it. There was a dude with Belgian waffles. He said they were fresh off the waffle iron. Jaime thanked him.

"We are going to Angela and Lionel's tonight for dinner," Jaime told me.

I nodded as I ate my waffles covered with thick, sweet pecan drizzle, crushed pecans, and caramelized bananas. Jaime reached for his coffee and sipped.

"We are going to meet up tomorrow morning at 8:00 a.m., go to the parade, then have dinner at their place."

"No," I said while shaking my head and reaching for my coffee.

Jaime raised his left brow.

I sipped my coffee and said, "Baby, last time I wore my pink peacoat, it got dirty. No way."

Jaime laughed like an evil super villain while rubbing his hands together.

"I know. Here," he said as he reached behind the couch and handed me a Macy's bag.

I took the bag and pulled out a North Face down jacket, black Ugg boots, and jeans.

"Thank you," I gushed.

"No problem. I have to go," Jaime said as he reached for his orange juice and sipped then used the cloth napkin to wipe the corners of his mouth.

"Where are you going?" I asked as he tossed a couple thousand dollars and a black credit card my way.

"I am going to help Lionel at the restaurant. I'll meet you back here at 3:00 p.m. Angela is meeting you for a spa day. Have fun," he said as he kissed my lips and dashed out.

I got an email reminder for my appointment at 1:00 p.m. Jaime called and said that Angela wanted to meet me at The Palm Court before then for tea. Sure. I turned off the television, showered, and dressed. I wore black sweats and a halter top, my hair was down, and I had on my diamond tennis bracelet, a platinum diamond necklace, and diamond earrings. I sprayed a little Givenchy Play on my neck and wrist, and I carried my Yves Saint Laurent purse.

"Ashanti," Angela called out when she saw me.

She wore all black; a diamond necklace, wedding ring, and earrings; and her long, black hair looked magnificent. Angela is a label whore. She fits in with this New York socialite crowd. She had her face, breasts, butt, and stomach done. All of her youthful looks were gone. But let me tell you this, she was the hottest thing walking up, down, and around Towson State University. Lionel and

Angela were a hot couple. I didn't recognize her because she looked different, but nothing changed the fact that she has a huge heart and she's very compassionate.

Angela had about four or five mixed drinks, and she kept the conversation live with her New York accent. I don't know where it came from, but it was thick and cute.

We talked about fashion, clothes, hair, and makeup. She asked about the real estate business and Pete's. I am sure Lionel keeps her informed about Pete's. Angela is one of our biggest clients. Each week she sends for chocolate treats for her clients and students at the fashion school.

Angela and I had the lox and bagels, scones, and black and white éclairs. Once lunch was over, we headed to the spa to have our spa day. We got massages, facials, mani-pedis, and we both got our hair done up nice. I love a good highlight job. Angela told me to go for the high-lights, low lights, and layers. I loved it. We also had tea and cake between services. Angela went tanning while I relaxed in the wind down room.

When it was time to pay, Angela rushed out of the tanning room with her black card in hand. She told the receptionist to tally up both of us, it was on her, and she told them to split a $400.00 tip. I had to purchase some products for my hair because the spa products felt noth-ing like the products I had at home.

Angela asked, "Want me to get it, Honey?"

"No, I got it," I said.

"Sure?" she asked.

"Yes," I laughed.

She fanned her hands and went to get dressed. It was a great first day in New York. I could not wait to see what my love had in store for me for the rest of the week.

Chapter Ten

∙∙∙∙∙∙∙∙∙∙ ∙ ∙∙∙∙∙∙∙∙∙∙

BOSS UP

I could not wait to get back to the room to tell Jaime about the experience I had at the spa. I felt like a queen. I could do this every day. It was around 4:30 p.m. when I got back. Jaime was on the bed stretched out, listening to Christmas music, and on the phone with his mom. I kissed his cheek. He smiled. I did not want to disturb him. I'm surprised he didn't say anything to me about coming back from the spa late.

I went to take a quick shower with the products I purchased from the spa. Jaime yelled from the bedroom that I smelled lovely and he was coming to join me. I had the water on full blast, so I didn't hear him when he entered the shower. When I felt him there, I turned to face him and offered him the sponge.

He said, "We don't have time, Baby, we got to hurry and go."

His mouth said one thing, but his hormones said another. He closed the shower door, lifted me up on his waist, then we took our time kissing and rubbing one another with the sponge. Then, one thing led to another and all I remember telling my husband was, "Don't mess up my hair."

Jaime said we had half hour to take a quick nap, then we had to head up to the Upper East Side. I nodded as I wrapped myself in my terry cloth robe and climbed into the king sized bed with satin sheets. I was out like a light.

It was 7:33 p.m. when we woke up. I couldn't do anything but brush my teeth, dress, and put on a thin layer of Chanel lip gloss. I like the pretty pink with sparkles. I managed to squeeze in a little foundation. The limo called as I was fixing my high bun with those kissed by the sun highlights. I put on my diamond earrings, bracelet, necklace, and wedding band. I didn't want to wear my diamond ring, so I put it in the safe in the room. I was ready to discuss fashion and talk with the elite. I was also ready for the million and one questions about how this black girl from the hood with all those diamonds on snagged this fine ass black man with all this money. I sprayed some Chanel Coco Mademoiselle on my wrist and neck and a little on my v-neck Zac Posen dress as I slid into my brand new glittered Christian Louboutin peep toe heels. I must've been out of my mind wearing those shoes that night, but I had to show off my pink pedicured toes.

On our way to Lionel's, Jaime and I talked about the upcoming holiday and all the plans he had for our future and Pete's. He said working with Lionel had allowed him to realize his childhood dreams and he wanted to take Pete's to the next level. We already had the Harbor, Annapolis, and Towson locations. I couldn't wait to see how far he wanted to go. If you could've seen the determination in his eyes, it would've warmed your heart. It was so awesome to be a part of Jaime's life as he lived out his dream. Tears welled up in my eyes as we pulled up in front of the lavish Upper East Side home. I wanted to cry, but I didn't want to smear my makeup.

Angela acted as if we had not seen one another a couple of hours earlier. She took my chinchilla and wrapped me up in her loving arms. She squeezed so tight. She smelt so good.

"I love the outfit," she said to me.

"Thanks."

"Who are you wearing?"

"Zac Posen," I responded.

I am new to this. I am what they call new money. Jaime is not new to this. He fit in perfectly.

Angela was so proud. You would've thought I had just graduated from Harvard Law School.

"Look at you," she gushed.

Jaime cleared his throat. Clearly, I was getting way too much attention.

"Oh, hello Jaime," Angela teased as they hugged one another. "Looking good brother."

Their house was fantastic with paintings straight from Paris, antique French furniture, Persian rugs, and crystal chandeliers. It was laid out from top to bottom. There was a seven-foot tall faux Christmas tree adorned with Tiffany blue ornaments and tinsel, candles, and blinking white lights. Angela's house made our condo look simple, and there is nothing simple about our condo.

Of course, we ended up in the kitchen where Lionel and his crew were cooking pumpkin soup, New York strip steaks, seafood risotto, loaded baked potatoes, lobster tails, and salad. There were also thick slices of New York style cheesecake. How fitting, right? There were people all over the place with trays of champagne with strawberries, cheese, fruit, chocolates, and shrimp cocktails. You name it. They had it.

Jaime pointed over to Lionel.

"He cooking?"

Angela nodded as she took a sip of champagne. She asked would I like a glass. I nodded and took a fresh flute from her hands.

"Of course. I can't get my man to touch me unless I'm wearing pots and pans. And if he's cheating, he's cheating with a recipe or a chick with a better kitchen," she teased.

"I know the feeling," I said.

"Listen, I have to go and mingle with the guests. You two have a good time. I'll see you at dinner," Angela said as she hurried off.

As a tall guy with a tray of crab balls walked past Jaime and me, I took a few, and bit into one of the golden brown balls.

"Bay... be," I said as I shoved one into Jaime's mouth.

Jaime chewed it up and said, "He learned a lot from me."

His chest rose into the air like a proud father. I shook my head and smiled.

Jaime and I walked closer to Lionel. There was so much going on that he didn't know, as he would say, that he was in the presence of greatness. Lionel's face lit up when we came into view.

"Hey," he said.

It warmed my heart to see the brothers embrace one another. It was a hug as if they hadn't seen one another hours ago. Lionel came from around the stove and gave me a big bear hug. I think he bruised my ribs.

"Angie said you two had a great time at the spa today."

"We did, thank you. Everything is beautiful."

"Thanks, Mrs. Harris."

"Hey, Man, do you need some help?" Jaime asked as he was taking off his jacket. "I can slice up the cheesecake."

"He won't stop," Lionel laughed.

I agreed.

"Listen," Lionel told Jaime, "you helped out a lot today. Go and enjoy yourself. Hey, we are leaving tomorrow at 7:00 a.m. I've lived here nineteen years and I've never been to the parade. I want to get good seats."

"Really?" I asked.

Lionel nodded. "Yeah." He swiped sweat from his brow. "You two go on and have a seat. I am taking care of you two tonight."

As Jaime and I left the kitchen holding hands, a butler escorted us to the dining area that was fit for kings and queens.

Jaime and I were seated next to the head of the table. We were given menus and asked if we would like a Caesar or house salad. Jaime told me to get the house salad. Lionel makes the dressing with anchovies. I didn't like the sound of it, but Jaime said to trust him. I had the pumpkin soup. Jaime had curried carrot soup. It was amazing. Everything was marvelous. The New York strip was so nice and tender, it tasted like butter. The shrimp risotto was out of this world. Jaime makes great risotto, but Lionel's takes the cake. It was smooth, rich, and creamy, just the way I like it. I ate so much I could not move.

Angela tapped the side of her wine goblet and caught the attention of the talkative table.

"To my friends," she said as the servers walked out with trays of brownies and placed them in front of everyone.

A few of the guests joked, asking where the vanilla ice cream was. Lionel sat back in the chair and kept his eye on Jaime. I picked up the moist piece of chocolate and took a bite. Lionel chuckled. It tasted familiar. After Jaime took a bite, he looked at Lionel and back at the brownie.

"These taste awfully familiar," Jaime joked.

Lionel stood at the head of the table and said, "Dude, I make those at my restaurant. They are like my bestseller."

Jaime lowered his head into his chest and laughed.

"When were you going to tell me?" he asked.

I devoured my brownie and I took Jaime's.

"I want you to partner with me," Lionel said as he walked around the table and caressed my shoulders. "I want you two to partner with me since it is your…"

"My aunt's recipe?" I asked as I swiped tears from the corners of my eyes.

"I can't keep those brownies on the shelf. People all over New York have been ordering them all winter. They fly during the holiday. I got a big-time order from a few friends that work over at the department stores," Lionel added.

"Is that how you got tickets to the parade tomorrow?" Jaime asked.

Lionel nodded and said, "I sold the recipe. Those brownies are going to be on the shelves by next holiday. We are going to talk to distributors Friday morning before you leave. It's my way of thanking you for all the hard work you put in and how you helped me over the years. Listen up folks…"

Lionel spoke up as if he didn't have our attention already. I couldn't stop tearing up.

He announced to all of the guests, "When I am in need of help, I call this guy and he drops everything to come help me. I love you guys. I always looked up to you. I still do."

Lionel reached into his back pocket and the table erupted in applause. Jaime didn't say a word. Lionel handed him a check. I looked over Jaime's shoulders. When I saw the amount, I took a sip of wine. I had never seen so many zeros before in my life. Angela was crying.

Jaime stood up and hugged Lionel. I grabbed my linen napkin, never mind the mess I made, and swiped my eyes. I was so overjoyed.

Lionel reached for his flute of champagne and said, "I would say welcome to the millionaire boys club, but you've been a member since birth."

The table erupted in laughter. Lionel and Jaime raised their glasses high and toasted to the good life. If Jaime didn't have Pete's, he could easily retire off of this business venture with Lionel.

The next morning, we went to the Macy's Thanksgiving Day parade. We had kickass seats right in front of Macy's in Herald Square. Jaime and I were cheek to cheek. It was cold. Angela had on her huge frames and held a thermos filled with wine. Afterwards, we did some shopping, went to Lionel's dad's restaurant for lunch, and then we had a huge feast at Lionel's restaurant with his staff in Scarsdale, New York. It was that holiday that catapulted my husband to millionaire status on his own from his hard work and determination.

Chapter Eleven

THE STORY OF US

Growing up, I was overlooked and talked about. Nobody wanted any of this until my husband locked me down. Jaime was my first love. He made me realize how beautiful and desirable I am. He would say, "Ashanti, Baby, you're so beautiful."

I believed him. No other man besides my father ever told me how beautiful I am. No man has ever looked at me the way Jaime has. That man looks at me as if I am the only woman in the room. He can enter a room with a million beautiful women and focus all of his attention on me.

He's my first. I wanted him to be my last. We've never broken up and if we have a disagreement, it is resolved by bedtime. I am not going to bed without kissing or making love to my husband. Now, there have been times when I have told him to sleep on the couch because he pissed me off and I told him to kiss my ass. But, he's back by my side before sunrise.

Jaime already knew what he wanted out of life way before he met me. So, imagine how I felt when his dragon lady Mama blamed me for Jaime's "lack of focus," as she put it. Jaime played football because his mother wanted him to play. He said his injury was his exit. Once he got better and was able to stand properly, he worked in kitchens.

His mother said, "That's what ghetto people do."

In the twenty years that Jaime and I have been together, I've only been blessed with her presences five times. She never came to anything Jaime had at the restaurant. And when he took money from his trust fund, she put a hold on his account. I asked him if that was legal. He said his mother can do whatever she damn well please. His mother gave him the blues.

Jaime's been all over the world and back. He has traveled to places that most have only dreamed of. Jaime does not let the color of his skin define him. He's fearless. I admire him. I wish his mother would've opened her heart up and accepted her son.

Before Jaime and I moved to New York, I attended Howard. Jaime worked at this steakhouse in DC. It was nice having him around. After culinary school, he traveled to Greece. I didn't go because I had school. Since I didn't come from money, I didn't want to jeopardize my scholarship. During my junior year, he was offered a job at Lionel's father's five-star Michelin restaurant in upstate New York. He didn't have to ask; I was ready to go with him and start my new life. I finished out the school year and two weeks after the semester ended, we packed and moved upstate. I didn't have a job, money, or finances to continue school the next semester, so I had to depend on him. He didn't mind putting up the money for my education. Unlike most girls that want bags, purses, and trips, I wanted an education. I didn't want to be a trophy wife.

I fit in in New York. I loved it. I actually miss it. I want to go back, get an apartment, and stay during the holidays. I worked at Macy's three days a week. Jaime bought me my first fully loaded Jeep Wrangler. It was a long commute. On a good day, it was two hours to get to the city. I didn't mind because Jaime worked morning, noon, and night. I only saw him on Sundays. He would come home worn out. I had school and work to tend to. We were like passing ships in the night. Sunday was family time. We took trips down to Manhattan. He was impressed. He never left Long Island. He didn't know I knew the city like I did. And when it snowed, watch out. I was nervous at first because Upstate, unlike Baltimore, does not shut down. We still have to go to work and school.

I remember when there was a storm in Baltimore that dumped eighteen inches of snow on the city. Mama was sick and had to go to the emergency room, but there was no one to take her. I got in my Land Cruiser and went to get my mother. I whipped through those streets and highways like it wasn't nothing on the ground. When I got her to the emergency room, the doctor asked could I go get some nurses that were stuck at home.

I was a true New Yorker. I caught the train with my friends and I walked through the Bronx and Queens with no fear. Jaime hated it. He said it was time to go home. I didn't want to leave. When I graduated from Syracuse, we went back home, and Jaime began working on Pete's.

♥

Pete's began as a catering business that took off within months. I was working by his side, taking phone calls, and sending out invoices. It was very exciting, and I was so proud of my Jaime. But, it became a bit overwhelming for the both of us.

Jaime made a lot of contacts while working in DC, New York, and abroad. He worked out of the study in his two-bedroom condominium, then it became a three-bedroom condo. He was running out of space.

Jaime's dad needed part-time help at the law firm. Instead of hiring and training someone, he asked me if I could work with him for a couple of hours a day answering phones and filing. His secretary was on maternity leave. She had been due back in six weeks, but it was going on eight weeks and she hadn't said anything about coming back.

"Excuse me."

I was at the office with Jaime Sr. early one Saturday morning, filing papers, returning emails, and listening to messages. We weren't expecting anyone. I thought I had locked the door behind me.

"Yes."

"I'm Dr. William Parker. I'm here to see Jaime. Are you Ashanti?"

Dr. Parker was charming. Thank you, black Jesus. I don't know if he was black, Hispanic, or what. All I knew was that he was fine as hell with the salt and pepper in his beard, and he was wearing the hell out of that Gucci suit and shoes.

I was flustered. I hung up the phone mid-message and brushed my hair away from my face.

"Yes, I am Ashanti," I responded.

He said, "I'm having a dinner for my parents' wedding anniversary. Jaime said that if he wasn't in, I should talk to you."

Jaime conducted his catering business from our condo and when he could not meet with someone, he sent them to his father's law firm. That was the first time I ever met with a client face to face.

"Sure. Come on over and have a seat."

I didn't have any catering invoices, so I grabbed a couple pieces of paper and a felt tip pen, and I led the fine ass young man over to one of the couches in the waiting area.

"We can go over some things," I said.

I'd never been flustered before in my life, but that man made me nervous. They say your replacement is closer than you think, but I had no idea that meeting that beautiful stranger would change the way I felt about the life that had chosen me.

♥

The next Saturday while working at the office with Jaime's dad, I met Russell Thompson. Russell and Jaime Sr. had been friends since law school. Russell passed away from lung cancer. He was smooth. He always had a cigar in one hand, shined cufflinks, and he always wore a three-piece suit with Italian leather shoes. He called me Dimples.

He said, "You always got a smile on that face when I walk in the door."

I would smile and say thank you.

"You plan on using that Syracuse education down here with this bum?" he teased.

"Here?" I asked.

He handed me a business card. His wife had a up and coming real estate school.

He said, "If you tell her I sent you, she will slash the price in half."

I'd heard that real estate school was expensive. I took the card and talked it over with Jaime.

Jaime looked at me with one brow in the air then laughed and said, "Sell houses, Baby." He continued, "You believe in me and I believe in you. Sign up for the classes and I got you. Open a business and I got you for life."

I nodded and said, "Yes."

I had no idea what I was getting into, but I knew it was the start of something wonderful. I studied hard and my social life was nonexistent. But I completed the classes, all while working with Jaime and his dad and going to school. I was a busy young lady. I knew what I wanted out of life, but I didn't know how all of it was going to come together. Once I completed real estate school, I got my license, and began working part-time with Russell's wife at her real estate firm. Rene took me under her wing. She could sell water to a whale. She is awesome. Everything I know, I owe to her.

One evening, Jaime, myself, his dad, and a few of his wealthy friends went to dinner at Ruth's Chris Steak House. While we were dining on those expensive cuts of meat, sipping champagne, and enjoying conversation, Jaime told his father that I finally graduated from real estate school. Jaime Sr. was impressed, but he was also a little upset because I couldn't work with him anymore.

Jaime Sr. was always on the go, he still is. His clients are drug dealers. Not those low-end ones either. They are the big time ones that need the Feds off their asses. There were dudes that used to come into the office with suitcases of cash. I had to count it and deposit it. Drugs dealers don't take receipts.

Bella Day Richards (one of the kingpin's wives that wears nothing but designer shoes, clothes, and diamonds; she drips) told me over dinner that her son was look-ing for a place to live. He's a dealer as well. I didn't know what to do, where to start, or even how to explain to that woman that I do not want to be involved with drug deal-ers. Jaime said it was okay and if I needed anything, just let him know. I was dumbfounded. I sold my first home for a quarter of a million dollars to a drug dealer. I got a beautiful commission check. Rene said I was a beast. I took that as a compliment. She bragged about me all around town, to her friends, and to her family. Two long years later, I opened my own real estate agency.

Chapter Twelve

LOVE DON'T NEED
A HOLIDAY

Jaime was never in the restaurant in the beginning. He had clients that had events and dinners that he had to cater to. So, he dipped in and out of the restaurant a couple of hours a day to make sure that everything was going as planned, then he would leave. Once he was able to multitask between the businesses, everything went accordingly, and we were able to see one another.

We had plenty of private parties and dinners when we first opened. Dr. Parker was and still is one of our favorite clients. He rented out the whole restaurant for his parents' wedding anniversary. We don't decorate the restaurant. We only supply the space and the food. Dr. Parker had a decorating team. I was impressed.

Dr. Parker came in the morning of that first event to make sure everything went according to plan. He said that over five hundred people were coming, so we accommodated him as much as we could. The entire Pete's staff was on board when they heard how much cash they would make.

"Ashanti," Dr. Parker called out.

He signed for the balloons and roses as I walked over to him. I could smell him before I reached him.

"Hey."

"I've been so busy, I haven't had breakfast. Would you like to have a cup of coffee with me?"

I smiled then nodded and agreed to sit with Dr. Parker for a cup of coffee. As soon as we sat down at the bar, I asked Nick for two cups of dark roast. Nick nodded and began working on the order.

"Everything is coming along great, Will," I said.

"Yeah. I want to thank you and Jaime personally for allowing this to happen. This is great. My parents are going to be surprised."

"I'm glad we could be a part of your event."

Nick sat two cups of steaming hot coffee in front of us, along with some sugar, cream, and honey. I thanked Nick and fixed my coffee. Will drank his coffee black.

"Well," I said, lifting my cup. Dr. Parker lifted his.

We looked at one another, clinked cups, and I said, "To friends."

Dr. Parker winked then sipped. My eyes widened as I turned away and sipped my coffee. Fix it Jesus.

I couldn't stay all night for the party. I had to get up and work with Mama because her bakery was really busy with incoming orders. After Halloween, she was busy. We always hired holiday help for the bakery and drivers for deliveries.

On my way home that night, Mama called and told me that she couldn't hire anyone this year due to insufficient funds. I asked Mama what was the problem. Why couldn't we hire at least two people for the holiday? We needed the help. Even if we hired someone until January, it would help out. I didn't understand.

Mama said that my father was spending money. I was infuriated. What the hell is wrong with him? My father had no business spending that money. Mama closed up early because she ran out of things. My father does not know anything about running a business. No one tells him how to preach in the pulpit on Sundays.

I hung up the phone with my mother and called my father. It was not a pleasant conversation. I laid his black ass out. He didn't get a word in edgewise because I let him have it. My father was dead set against my mother opening her business. He had the nerve to tell my mother that he didn't want anything to do with it. So now she's doing better than you thought she would and you want to be a part of it? Bullshit, no the hell you are not.

I told him I would appreciate it if he would mind his business. Mama had to turn away her regular customers because my father skimped on products. Come to find out my mother was upset with me for laying Daddy out. Mama said I shouldn't talk down to my father.

I told her, "Mama, I work side by side with Jaime and I don't mean to sound rude or disrespectful but we make way more money and have a larger budget than your bakery."

She didn't respond.

I thought it would be a good idea to make dinner for Jaime and me. We hadn't seen one another in a while.

I made New York sirloin smothered in caramelized Vidalia onions, peppers, mushrooms; loaded mash and asparagus dipped in hot butter; and packaged chocolate cake for dessert. Jaime wanted sex after dinner, but my stomach was too full. There was no way in hell I was getting up on a dick and riding it tonight. Plus, I wasn't feeling well. I didn't finish my food and the wine didn't taste right.

Jaime and I cleared the table. He said he had to go over the holiday budget. Holiday budget? *Didn't we just go over the budget?* I wondered to myself, but I said nothing. He's the owner. If he wants to go over everything with a fine-tooth comb, I understand. I kissed his cheek and finished the dinner dishes.

When I was done, I went into the bedroom with Jaime. He was at the desk on his laptop and on the phone. I kissed his cheek and went into the bathroom to take a hot shower. I was tired but I needed it.

When I got out of the shower, I put on lotion and my favorite pink pajamas. Jaime was still on the phone. I got in the bed and made myself comfortable.

He laughed and said, "Yeah, see you in a few."

I looked at my watch. It was after 9:00 p.m.

I reached for my laptop and placed it on my lap.

"Who was that?" I asked as I logged in.

Jaime closed his laptop.

"A friend from college."

"Do I know them?" I asked, not taking my eyes off my laptop.

Jaime shook his head no. "I'm going out for a few."

"Jaime." We locked eyes. "It's almost 10:00 p.m."

"Baby, I'll be back." He walked into the bathroom and closed the door. I jumped out of bed and checked his laptop. My husband had never caused me to be suspicious, until then. I checked his emails. He had gotten an email from… oh shit. Rachael.

Rachael looks like the twins from *Sister Sister*. Well, the twins look better. Jaime had sent an email to Rachael, and she had immediately emailed him back and asked if it was ok for her to call him. He had replied yes.

I sat on the edge of the bed, cried, and thought to myself, *This cannot be happening. Why is this happening? Why am I getting emotional over a meeting? Calm down. It's ok.*

Jaime came out of the bathroom fully dressed. He sprayed Jean Paul Gaultier on his wrist, kissed my forehead, and left.

I texted Altovise and Elliott. I needed to see my family. I didn't sleep well at all that night.

The next day, we decided to meet up at Della's. I love Della's lobster bisque. I couldn't wait to get a bread bowl filled to the rim with that thick, sweet soup with chunks of lobster floating on top.

When I showed up at Della's, I was not expecting to see Jordan sitting at the table. Why would my sister invite Jordan out to dinner when I specifically told her that I needed to talk? Sometimes I wonder about my sister. Of course, Jordan was on her cell phone talking to Pam. Altovise loves drama and chaos. If something is going smoothly, she has to interrupt it. She will take a situation and pump it up to be worse than it is. She makes a mountain out of a mole hill. She's terrible. She's my sister and I love her, but I don't have to like her.

Elliott stood up and gave me a warm embrace. He whispered in my ear that he was over Jordan. I snickered as I sat down across from Altovise. I smiled at Jordan. Altovise was sipping on water. She couldn't look me in the damn face; she was so into the menu. I wanted to snatch it from her hands and hit her over the head with it. I didn't know what my sister was up to or what the hell I had walked into, but I did not like it.

We ordered waters, lemonade, and oysters for apps. I stared at the menu. I knew what I wanted, I just wanted to be an ass.

"So," Jordan said as she leaned over the table. "Rachael is in town for the holidays."

Altovise rolled her eyes as she snacked on a kale salad. If looks could kill, Jordan would've been dead. Now, all of the sudden, my sister was irritated with her.

"She's a Delta like you Altovise," Jordan continued on.

Altovise exhaled loudly and shook her head. Jordan looked over at Altovise and snickered.

"She went to Morgan. Didn't you two pledge together?" Jordan asked as she dumped salt and hot sauce on her oysters.

Before Altovise even had a chance to answer, Jordan continued, "She dated Jaime while you two were on a break."

"Jaime and I never went on a break," I said. "He proposed when I graduated from high school."

I had the bread bowl of lobster bisque in front of me with a glass of frosted lemonade. I was sick.

Jordan's mouth hit the table. At that moment, she knew she had fucked up. I had enough. I told her to spill her guts.

She said, "I heard they went on a couple dates, and she wore his letter jacket and drove his car."

The entire restaurant got silent as if they wanted to hear the rest of the story. It was eerily quiet; you could hear a pin drop.

"Maybe it was innocent," Elliott said, breaking the awkward silence in the restaurant.

And just like that, everyone began talking.

Altovise sipped her wine and asked for another bottle.

"Wow." Tears filled my eyes. I excused myself from the table and went to the bathroom.

I held onto the toilet bowl and threw up. There was a knock on my stall door.

"Are you okay?" Altovise asked.

I opened the stall door. Altovise brushed my hair away from my shoulders and I fell into her arms and cried, "He lied to me."

"Come on." She led me over to the sink. "Why get upset over something that happened twenty years ago?"

"He went out with her last night," I said.

Altovise's eyes widened.

"I did not want him to go," I cried.

I had waited up for Jaime. He came in around 2:00 a.m. He was singing and dancing. He walked over to the bed and shook me. He said he was going to take a shower, but he had already taken a shower before he left. I rolled over and watched him undress. His dick was rock hard. So, when he came out of the shower glistening and smelling good, I climbed from the bed and wrapped my lips around his dick. He grabbed the back of my head and guided it. He let out a few moans and groans to let me know I was doing a good job.

"I don't know what to do," I said to my sister. "All of these crazy thoughts are running through my head like what if they did it or what if he stopped her and he came home and finished with me? I really don't feel good."

"I'm sorry."

"He woke up before me and left before I had a chance to say bye."

"Wow."

"I know right."

"Mama always says, 'Go with your heart, Love.' Jaime loves you."

"Well, love's in need of love. Love is hurting."

Chapter Thirteen

LOVE'S THE START OF OUR HOLIDAY

After lunch, Altovise and I headed to the drug store to get a pregnancy test, two Snickers bars, Doritos, and a bottle of Snapple. I am a regular, twenty-one-day girl. I didn't tell Jaime that my period was a couple weeks late. I asked Altovise to be there with me when I took the test. Jordan went to work. Elliott headed to the church to help with our Thanksgiving dinner for the homeless.

I changed into a pair of jeans and a sweater once we got back to the condo. Altovise grabbed some ice cream and chocolate cake. I went to pee on the sticks. I had purchased three. And would you believe it, all three came back positive.

I walked out of the bathroom and showed Altovise the sticks. She stood up, took them, smiled, and said, "I'm going to be an aunty."

She took me in her arms and held me tightly.

Then she broke away and teased, "This explains your moody ass."

I went to take a nap. I don't know what Altovise was doing. The ringing of the doorbell woke me up. Altovise walked out of the kitchen with another slice of chocolate cake and two mounds of vanilla bean ice cream. I rubbed my eyes and went to answer the door. As I approached it, my stomach dropped. I felt cold. I reached for the knob and turned. It was the dragon lady. I was staring evil in the face. Altovise jumped up from the couch.

Jaime's mother was so dramatic. She had on a floor length chinchilla and she was batting her long, ugly lashes.

"Ashanti, is Jaime in?"

"No, he's not. Would you like to come in?" I asked.

She let out a long, heavy, dramatic sigh then rolled her eyes. My heart hurt. What did I do to this woman?

"No," she said as she shot a dagger that hurt worse than a bullet.

She knew how to push a button and she pushed it well with those long ass claws she called nails. "I just came to see him. Rachael and I are out and about. She's down in the limo."

I had all I could take.

"You know her?" I asked.

But, what I really wanted to ask was if her father the devil missed her because for a woman as beautiful as her, she's ugly, and she has a condo in hell.

"No, Mrs. Harris, I do not know her."

Then the bitch got this sneaky, ugly ass, sly grin on her face like the Grinch when he tried to steal Christmas.

She moved in and said, "Of course I do, they dated in high school and college."

I stood there for a hot second and inhaled.

"Fuck you," I said as I slammed the door. The security guard called up and asked me if I was ok. I told him I wasn't. He must've seen the commotion go down on the surveillance camera at the front desk.

I met Jaime's parents in 1993 and it's been pure hell since then. His father is a wonderful man and he's very generous. His mother was always a piece of work. A year after Jaime and I returned to Baltimore, she had dinner at this expensive seafood restaurant at the Harbor, but she only invited Jaime. He didn't bother to tell me about it until later because he didn't want to hurt my feelings. But I was hurt.

Mrs. Harris did not attend our engagement party. Altovise said she sent her an invitation. Jaime said that his mother did not receive an invite; she was so hurt that she went on vacation to Aruba to get away from it all.

She told Jaime that she didn't want to come to the wedding. Jaime sat on the edge of the bed and cried. I didn't know what to do. I stood there and watched him break down like a child that had lost a parent. That was the straw that broke the camel's back. I was already going through it with my miscarriage and here this bitch came with the rudeness. I told Jaime that I was not going to reach out to that dragon lady ever. She didn't have to come. And since she said she didn't want to come, I didn't want her there.

Jaime's father said he had enough of the unnecessary nonsense. He said he was going to have a talk with her. Jaime told his father that he did not have to because she would've made it about her and it's our wedding day.

Jaime's father made her come to our wedding and the bitch wore black. She looked nice. My cousin said she overheard Mrs. Harris telling people that she paid for everything. I said it was true. She had given Jaime money, but she did not have to go around telling people that she'd just met and would never see again in her ratchet life that she paid for everything.

Mrs. Harris was hate filled, spiteful, and malicious. There was not a good bone in that woman's body and I never got a chance to talk to her about anything or even ask her how it felt to be that evil. If you were on fire, she would roast marshmallows and make S'mores or rub her hands together to get warm. She would pour gasoline on you to make the fire bigger just so that she could be warm. She would toss ice water on you in the winter. She would laugh when you fall and wouldn't offer to pick you up. If she had the last loaf of bread and she was full but you were hungry, she would throw it away. Do you get where I'm coming from?

I had enough of being disrespected. Altovise told me to calm down for the baby's sake. For a second, I had forgotten about my baby. Altovise made some tea while I calmed down and finished packing a couple of outfits. Then I placed my bag by the door.

"Hey, Baby, I got you some chicken and kale salad," Jaime said as he walked into our condo. He finally showed up after I had texted him a million times.

"Your mom and Rachael came by," I said.

"What?"

"I want to know what's going on."

"Baby," he exhaled. He saw my bags. "Ashanti…"

He shook his head as if he were the one that was tired of the bullshit. I was fed up and tired of the drama. I wanted out. I didn't care what it cost. Sometimes your piece of mind is worth all the riches in the world.

"I have to go."

I threw one of the pregnancy tests at him and walked towards the front door.

Chapter Fourteen

FOR MY LOVE

I didn't feel like going to the gym after work. My body was sore from working a twelve-hour shift. I worked thirty-six hours in three days and still had a couple days left until my weekend. I was worn out. I didn't want to wake Ashanti. After the night I had with Rachael and the crew, I woke up, took a quick shower, and was out the door.

There is nothing like the smell of fresh coffee in the morning. Before I left to start my day, I had a cup of hot coffee and a hot croissant with butter. I prefer to make them myself. When I am bored, I bake. So, I had already baked a couple dozen and frozen them. I bag them individually and when I am ready to eat them, I heat and serve. I love the quiet and stillness of the morning. 5:00 a.m. is my favorite time. I appreciate Mother Nature. When we were younger, Pops used to take Pete, Red, Felix, and yours truly camping. I was always the first one up. I would sit by the river; watch the sun rise between the trees; and listen to the birds, wind, and river ripple.

I was on my way out the door when I received a call from Mother Bond.

"Yes, Love," I answered as I stepped outside into the warm hallway.

"Jaime, our dinner for the homeless is tonight. Pastor changed the date. Can I get two pans of your macaroni and cheese?"

She asked so sweetly, I could not say no.

"Everyone loves it and it was a complete success last year," she continued.

I chuckled. The homeless had gotten some but Altovise and the crew had made plates before everyone arrived.

I'd said to myself, *What kind of hood, ghetto shit is that?*

I told Mother Bond that Felix would deliver the two pans of macaroni and cheese. Before I got to work, I called and asked Felix if we had enough to make them.

Felix said, "Fuck you."

I laughed out loud.

"Dude, we are down here making fucking homemade cranberry sauce for your ass. My fingers are red as fuck and I'm tired as fuck," he said.

I went to the grocery store and grabbed everything I needed to make Mother Bond the macaroni and cheese. As I walked into the restaurant, Whitney Houston's "Do You Hear What I Hear" played overhead.

"Man, what the fuck are you doing?" Demetrius asked as he wobbled into the kitchen.

It was the Tuesday before Thanksgiving and everyone was on deck. The doors to the sweethearts booth open at 7:00 a.m. We had a pre-dessert sale that went from 7:00 a.m. until 12:00 p.m. I say pre-event because the actual event is Wednesday morning. It's a preview of what we will serve. I am excited every year. We gross so much money this time of year that we're good from one Thanksgiving to the next. I have bakers that drive luxury cars. The baked goods are that good and you know the money is excellent.

We close at 12:00 p.m. in preparation for the thousands of baked goods that go out the following day. I have a staff of over thirty bakers getting thousands of orders out. We start baking at 12:00 p.m. and we don't stop until we close on Thanksgiving Eve at 9:00 p.m. Everyone is dead ass tired, but it is worth it.

"I am making my mother-in-law some macaroni and cheese."

"That's tonight?" he asked.

I nodded as I sipped my coffee.

"Well, three people not here," he said.

My heart dropped.

"Who?" I asked as I gathered my ingredients.

I was not surprised though. We were slammed yesterday. Most of these young cats can't handle this pressure but they love the money. I understand. If I wasn't the boss, I would've called out too.

"Well, Sam, Brit, Nia, and Monica are on the way. Van is coming in. Stephan and Gisselle are downstairs. I think Betty, Tina, and Augusta called out."

"Augusta is pregnant. Where is Belle?"

"In the office."

"I'll be out of your way in an hour. Monica is supposed to prep."

"I know. Felix is doing the cranberry sauce. Juan is here. He's making the turkeys."

"Cool. Sounds like everything is going well." I was happy that the crew that was there was picking up the slack for the staff that had called out.

"We got it, Boss. We got a huge order going out at 12:00 p.m."

"How many?"

"150. I'm gonna start that at 8:00 a.m. It's cold sandwiches, chips, and drinks. I got the new girl rolling pickles. We should be done in about an hour then PJ is running it over with Red."

"Make sure those two come back. I heard they were smoking on the way to deliveries."

"I got you, Boss."

♥

The morning flew by so fast that by the time I had a chance to sit down, it was the start of the lunch rush.

"How much longer on table six?" I asked the line.

Belle was expediting. Table six had been waiting a while.

"We got slammed at lunch," she said. "We ran out of crab cakes."

We ran out of crab cakes. Really? When Belle told me that I laughed. How? Are they that good? Are we that popular? It felt good to run out of stuff. I didn't feel like making any more. I had prepped over a hundred before I left the night before. Crab cakes are my specialty. No one preps them but me. I trust you to cook them but never prep. The staff knows when I prep them. My wife can look at them in the fryer, smell them, and know.

She will say, "Jaime didn't prep these."

I took down the special then ran into the office and printed out some flyers to put inside of the menus. I asked Felix if they had enough buffalo wings for a special. He nodded and swiped sweat from his brow. I hurried downstairs with the flyers and told the hostess to put them inside of the menus. She took the stack and did as she was told. I hurried back upstairs to help out. Two days before the holiday, I always run specials. We had a crab cake, french fries, coleslaw, and chocolate cake for $20.00. It flew. All my food is cooked to order. I don't have nothing sitting around under a light. And forget about a microwave. There's none on the line.

Our Thanksgiving special is roasted turkey with dressing, mashed potatoes and gravy, macaroni and cheese, green beans or collards, homemade cranberry sauce, and a roll. We're closed Thursday but we run the turkey special all day on Wednesday. We also have turkey salad, open faced turkey sandwiches, turkey on a house salad, and stone mill grits and shrimp with a poached egg all day. We also serve the regular Pete's menu, but it's limited. We reopen on Black Friday for dinner at 4:00 p.m.

All I wanted to do was go home and relax with my wife, but it was hectic at work as always. Around 6:00 p.m., I made a huge deposit, picked up wagyu steaks, and headed home. I could not wait to get there. Ashanti was a tad moody, but I knew dinner would make her happy. She had gone through so much trouble the day before making dinner for me, I thought I would return the favor. Dinner would be later than usual, so being the loving husband that I am, I grabbed her a kale salad to hold her over until it was ready.

As soon as I stepped inside of the condo, we got into an argument. We had been arguing a lot. I tried to make my wife happy the best way I know how––by showering her with gifts. That was what I was taught as a child. My mother and father weren't there for me as they should have been. They were extremely busy people. Instead, they compensated me with gifts. It was a competition for my affection and my father won hands down. My mother didn't like that. So, instead of embracing me, she pushed me away, and became the evil woman I grew to love. I never understood her and it was heartbreaking because I am nothing like her. As much as I loved her, I didn't feel the way she did about putting people down who didn't have as much as us. As far as Ashanti being upset, I had no idea what was going on, but I knew my mother was a part of the drama.

I picked up the positive pregnancy test that she had thrown at me. Then, I watched as she struggled with her bags. I'm no punk bitch, but I got down on my hands and knees, cried, and begged her to stay. I was so hurt it hit Altovise. She stood there with tears in her eyes watching it all go down, and it takes a lot for her to become emotional. I didn't want Ashanti to leave, especially since she was carrying my child. We had already lost one baby. I could not go through that again. She told me to stay away from her.

After Ashanti and Altovise left, I sat on the edge of the bed and held my head in my hands. I must've cried for over an hour. Then I called her, but she didn't answer, so I called her mother. I wish my mother embraced me the way Ashanti's family did. Since day one, they'd shown me nothing but love.

I had all I could stand. I didn't want to sit in the house feeling sorry for myself. So, I dried my tears, washed my face, changed my clothes, and made my way over to the church. Altovise was on the front stoop smoking. She has no damn class. I parked my BMW behind Ashanti's Benz.

Altovise walked towards my car.

"Spying? Stalking?" she asked as she tossed the cigarette to the side.

I got out of the BMW and Altovise and I leaned against it. I was afraid to walk into the church. "How far along is she?"

Altovise shrugged her shoulders. "I don't know." She exhaled. "She been sick all day. Are you coming in to help or are you going to pussy foot out here?"

Tita, the deacon and Altovise's best friend, greeted us at the front door. Let me tell you this, I'd never heard of a smoking and Amsterdam Pineapple drinking deacon before him. He was cool. I fucks with him. His wife is a cook. I would love for her to work with us at Pete's. There were a few homeless families inside having dinner. It smelled so good.

I couldn't keep my eyes off Ashanti. Altovise told me that I'd hurt Ashanti by going out with Rachael. I didn't know that seeing Rachael would hurt her. Then, it hurt me that my mother added fuel to the fire by going over to the condo and rubbing it in Ashanti's face. Rachael was not worth my marriage.

The banquet hall in the church's basement filled up fast with the less fortunate. This was my area of expertise. I am always down for helping and lending a hand when it's needed. I told Mrs. Bond that I was making a monetary donation to the church to help provide the homeless and less fortunate with the supplies, clothes, and food they would need during the holiday season. She said that everything helps and was so grateful that she made an announcement over the loudspeaker. The hall erupted in applause and whistles. Ashanti rolled her eyes up in her head and tapped her foot on the floor. She was done with me.

I helped out in the kitchen. It was just like expediting in the restaurant. The servers wore plastic gloves and hats, just like in the restaurant, and scooped out nice portions to the hungry crowd.

Mama and Elliott were making plates for the sick and shut in. Jillian, Tita's wife, told me that they were making rounds in the morning before the actual Thanksgiving dinner. She asked me did I want to come. I didn't know what to say. I was thinking about my baby.

I finally got a break and asked Altovise where Ashanti was. She said Ashanti was in the kitchen washing dishes. I thanked her and headed to the kitchen. Ashanti was the only one in there. This was my chance to talk to her and try to smooth everything over. I stood next to her at the sink. She cut her eyes at me and stopped washing the dishes.

"I'm staying at Mama's house. I'll come by the condo tomorrow to get my things."

"No, Love, Thanksgiving is tomorrow."

"Jaime," she sighed.

"I will leave. You can stay, Baby."

I took her hands in mine. She stood in front of me fighting tears.

"I want you to be happy," I said as I leaned in for a kiss.

She closed her eyes and puckered.

"Hey!" Felix burst through the kitchen doors with trays. "What up?" he asked as he walked over to the double basin where Ashanti and I were.

"Did I?" he asked as Ashanti walked away.

"As always," I laughed.

"Wanna go to the club tonight?" Felix winked. "You know who is going to be there, plus it's half off bottles."

"I don't think so."

"Come on, I will pick you up at 10:00 p.m."

"Okay, cool," I said with my shoulders in the air.

What harm would it do?

Chapter Fifteen

~~~~~~~~~ • ~~~~~~~~~

CARAMEL

She is sexy as fuck. I watched as she twirled her ass up and down that pole. She was fucking me without touching me. We locked eyes. We stayed up on one another all night.

What the fuck is wrong with you, Man? I thought to myself. *You have a beautiful, pregnant wife at home and you out here chasing stripper pussy? But, she relaxes me when I am having a rough day. I don't have to explain my whereabouts to her. I don't have to shower her with gifts. I don't even have to call her when I get home. All I do is whip the dick out and she takes care of me. I love my wife, but I need to release.*

I been dealing with this chick on and off for the past ten years, just as long as I been married. She's beautiful, black, and Dominican with the biggest ass ever. I paid for her breasts. I told her I was married. She plays her position and plays it well. Just to cover it up, I introduced her to Chance. Soon after that, six months into their relationship to be exact, Chance and Carmelita got married. I thought that after having him in her life, she would leave me alone. But, we still can't stay away from one another. It's not like Chance out here being faithful to her. He has his side pieces too and he treats them well.

"How you feeling?" she asked as she placed a shot of Bourbon in front of me. I took the glass, downed it, then slammed the empty glass on the bar. She took a shot and placed the glasses behind the bar.

"I'm okay. She's pregnant."

"So, what does that mean?" she asked, as she poured two more shots of Bourbon. "We falling back on one another?"

I lowered my head into my hands.

"Where the fuck are Felix and Red?"

"In the back getting their dicks sucked," she said and laughed as the bartender placed two more drinks down on the bar.

It was crowded and funky. All the girls were trying to get close to me, but I wasn't paying anyone any attention. I wasn't paying who I came to see any attention. I was missing my wife, but I wanted to feel the inside of her mouth.

"Destiny is back there. She got some coke."

"You know I don't do that shit," I said as I downed the second drink. "You can go on and have fun. I'm headed out."

"You don't want me to go with you?" she asked.

"No." I tossed a hundred-dollar bill on the bar. "I'm good."

♥

Caramel was upset. I told her that once I introduced her to my man it was over between us. I couldn't hurt the people

that I love anymore. If Chance found out that I was fucking his woman, he would murder my ass. Her real name
is Carmelita and she's dangerous. Her own stepmother
brought her into the stripping game. The club I just left
is owned by this gay dude and he said from the jump he
knew she was a money maker. Carmelita makes money
on and off the stage. The bitch fucks men and women
during her act. It's like watching porn in real time. I bet
you're wondering why the fuck I would want a woman
like that. A woman that has traveled all over the world to
suck international dick and made more money than me,
and I own several successful restaurants. It's a fantasy that
I allowed into my real life and it fucked me up severely. I
have watched this woman shoot up after she blew me off.
She loves to snort coke. She did dope back in the day with
Wes and Misha when she was a teenager. The sad part is
that I have given this girl a chance because Mila is her
sister. I told Carmelita I want her to change.

She said, "Fuck you, Jaime."

I had so much pent up rage that I hit her. I smacked
her four times in a row. That almost killed me. I had never
hit a woman before, but she was bothering me. I told her
to leave me alone, but she kept pushing my buttons. I
know I sound like a monster and she didn't deserve that.
I know that there were other ways of getting her to stop
doing drugs and whoring herself out to men, but in that
moment, I thought that maybe smacking the shit out of
her would do it. There is no reasoning with her though.

I stumbled outside to the Range and started the car. The Temptation's "Jingle Bells" came on. I couldn't see. I didn't want to go anywhere until my buzz wore off. I had a long ride ahead. Shit, I laughed as I pulled off into the night, the club wasn't that far from my condo I had that overlooked the marina. I texted Juan and his cutie to let him know I had dipped out. We all went there to have some serious fun, but once my fun was done, I was ready to go.

♥

I turned the doorknob on the condo door.

"Shit," Pops said while he pulled his robe together.

A beautiful brown skin honey jumped to her feet.

"Do you knock?" he asked.

"Nigga, I live here," I said as I laughed and closed the door.

"How did you get in?" I asked as I watched the brown skin honey grab her robe.

She was built like a stallion with that big bubble ass.

"I let myself in. I do have a key," I said while plopping down on the couch.

"Can you go in your room, Jaime?" Pops asked. "We are not finished."

"Excuse us, Sweetheart," I said as I smiled at the brown skin honey. She smiled back. She was beautiful.

She nodded as she strutted into the bedroom and closed the door.

"She been here before obviously," I said as I made my way over to the stocked mini bar.

Pops had the music low, candles burning, and Moët & Chandon on ice. I made myself a flute. "What about your wife?" I asked him.

"You know we not fucking. She's sick."

I gulped down my drink and nodded.

"Cancer came back?" I asked.

"She talking about she's not getting chemo this time. She wants to die. I said, 'Satan don't want you down there.'"

Pops and I giggled.

"Shit."

I stepped behind the bar. I forgot to mention that my father loves to spend time in my condo. His ass should pay some bills. It's cool though. He makes sure the bar stays filled with nothing but the best. I have an $8,000.00 bottle of Louis XIII Magnum. I've been holding onto that bottle since I was twenty-one years old. We only sip it. I grabbed two glasses and filled enough for the two of us.

"Cheers." Pops sipped. "Damn."

He stood up from the bar and danced in his silk, biscuit beige robe.

"That's that shit," he said.

I nodded as I sat on the leather couch in front of the faux fireplace.

Then he asked, "Problem?"

I shrugged as I grabbed one of those chocolate covered strawberries from the table.

"Ashanti is pregnant."

"I heard," Pops said as he sat across from me. He crossed his legs and sipped once more. "You happy?"

"Pop, I'm still fucking home girl from the club."

Pops shook his head in disgust.

"I told you about her. She's not the kind of woman you leave your wife for."

"Who then, Pop?"

"Shit mutha fucker, Beyoncé. You got more money than Jay-Z." Pops giggled. "I always told you that if you were going to step out on Ashanti, not that I encourage the shit, but step your game up. You don't do that to a woman like Ashanti. You don't fuck around on her with a woman like Carmelita. Son, she snorts dope and sucked and fucked all of Baltimore. That's not a good look for you."

"I love my wife. I do but... I don't know if I want to bring a child into the mix of my bullshit. I'm never home. I work like shit. I'm always tired."

"She happy?" Pop asked.

"Oh fuck yes."

I leaned back on the couch and chewed the strawberry. It was sweet. The chocolate was smooth and decadent.

"And you drinking?" Pop asked.

"Like a fish," I answered.

I downed the Louis and slammed the glass on the table.

"Mama is impossible," I said.

"You don't say. Why you think I'm knocking down anything that walks? For kicks?" he asked. "Your mother and I are done. I told her I was finished."

"What'd she say?"

"Fuck off."

I laughed. "That's Mama."

"Well, are you having dinner tomorrow at your place?"

"I can whip up something. Come over around 5:00 p.m."

"Cool. I got some business to take care of."

"Do your thing, Pop."

Before I knew it, I was knocked out.

♥

"I don't give a flying fuck!"

I exhaled as I woke up to racket. It was my father and Rosie arguing. I sat up and rubbed my eyes. Rosie is my mother's fast talking, sassy ass, Dominican housekeeper and best friend. She's the only one that can tolerate my mother's nonsense.

"Fuck you," Rosie screamed.

"First of all, who let you in?" Pop asked.

He was fully dressed.

"I got a key," Rosie said as she made her way into the living room where I was lying down.

I shook my head.

"Hey, Love," she said as she moved towards me for a kiss. "You drinking again?"

"Like a fish," Pop said. Then added, "Look, be gone before I get back."

Rosie gave Pop the finger as he left the condo.

"What'd I do to deserve this visit?" I asked as I walked into the kitchen.

Rosie followed me. I poured myself a cup of coffee and sipped.

"Yuck."

The coffee was thick, cold, and gross.

"Your father made it. Let me make breakfast." Rosie joined me in the kitchen. "Coffee?" she asked.

I nodded as I sat at the counter.

"Your mother is sick," Rosie added.

"I heard," I said as I rubbed my head.

"You coming over tonight?" she asked as she made coffee and gathered ingredients for omelets and raisin toast. I shook my head. I wasn't in the mood for the drama. "Your mother is having dinner catered. I get the day off. I'm actually going to New York this weekend."

"To see the fam?" I asked.

"I miss my babies."

She smiled as she diced the onions, jalapeño peppers, and green peppers.

"I haven't seen Cheryl and Lisa in ten years. They call though."

"I've seen Cheryl," I laughed.

Rosie shook her head and exhaled.

"What?" I asked innocently.

"Don't think I don't know about you two the summer before she went to college," Rosie laughed as she whipped the eggs.

She put a little cayenne pepper, salt, pepper, and garlic powder in the egg mixture then placed the bowl to the side. It smelled really good, but I was not in the mood to eat.

"She said you were her first love."

"I believe her."

Cheryl drove me crazy. She had the fattest ass. She was loose back there too. But I can't fuck with a chick with a loose booty hole. Her pussy looked like ground beef and she was hallowed. I'm very well endowed, but it was like tossing a hotdog down the hall. She was a mess. She gave good head though. Niggas wasn't lying when they said she was the best in town. She swallows your dick and balls. She needs to put her shit up on camera. She will make millions.

She had the nerve to call me a couple summers ago and ask me could I come up. I passed.

"Did she ever marry that dude she was dating?" I asked as if I gave a damn. I'm glad if she did.

"Unfortunately, yes," Rosie said as she sautéed the vegetables. "Marco. He's a good guy. I think he's sweet but he's ugly. He looks like a chimpanzee. A white one."

We laughed.

"Ashanti is pregnant."

"Yes. News travels fast."

"Baltimore is small. There's only two degrees of separation. I swear."

"Are you going home to your wife?" Rosie asked me. "She needs you."

"I know. I don't think I'm ready though."

"Jaime, come on. You are going to make a great Dad."

"I just hope I don't turn out like my dad."

"You won't."

"Then why don't I want to go see my mother or my pregnant wife?" I asked as I walked out of the kitchen and into my bedroom where I laid down. There was a knock on the door. "Yes."

Rosie stepped inside. "Hey, I am going to finish making breakfast. Then I am heading out. Your mother misses you, Jaime. She doesn't know better when it comes to matters of the heart. She thinks that Ashanti isn't good enough for you. But, I have told her on numerous occasions, you cannot help who you fall in love with."

"I don't miss her," I said.

"She doesn't have long left," Rosie said. I exhaled loudly. "Make the time she has left count."

"Thanks, Rosie. I love you, but you know the way out."

"Happy holidays, Love."

Chapter Sixteen

SWEET SIXTEEN

I was the shit in college, or at least I thought I was. Chicks used to scream my name whenever I walked into a room or across the football field. Even when I didn't have my gear on and I was not playing, I had my own cheering section. I loved that, but I also loved her. I was engaged to the most beautiful girl at Howard. Most of my admirers knew that I was engaged, but they didn't care. They still wanted me to meet them at the hotel or at their place. It took great strength to ignore them. I did not want to lose Ashanti. I didn't want to do anything to hurt her.

My mother and father both graduated from Morgan State. My mother was spoiled and entitled. She longed for nothing. Mama was born into royalty. I don't know much about my grandparents. All I know is that my mother inherited everything when they passed. My mother handled all of my bills. She would rather I sell drugs than cook.

Rachael and Ashanti share a mutual friend, Jordan. Jordan is closer to Rachael than she is to Ashanti. Rachael and Ashanti come from two different worlds. Rachael is a part of my mother's circle. Ashanti is the big butt, beautiful, curvy, ghetto girl. She has a big, soft ass and her eyes are hazel. I get lost in her eyes. No other woman has ever made me feel the way Ashanti does. She's everything. Sometimes, I think, she's a little too good for me.

Jordan and Rachael needed a place to stay. Sanaa, their sorority sister, called me. She was the go between. Jordan and I have always been cool. When I met her, we clicked. She loves football and Brandy. She used to smoke cigars with the fellas and sipped cognac. I would've given Jordan a chance, but she talked way too much.

I didn't want to see them on the streets, so I rented out my apartment to them. Mind you, Mama was paying my rent, so I was subleasing it to them. I only charged them $100.00 a month.

It was my last night in town before I headed to my chef job in DC. Rachael came into my room and one thing led to another. That was the last time I saw her.

While Ashanti and I were living in New York, Jordan asked had I seen or talked to Rachael. I said no. It was a one-time thing. The day after we slept together, Rachael moved out. Jordan said she would pick up the extra $100.00.

I said, "No problem. Don't worry about Rachael's share."

That was that.

♥

I finally went to see Mama.

"Hey, Baby," she said as she opened the door. It was weird cause she never does anything as simple as answering the door. Rosie was always there to answer the door, answer the telephone, and basically tend to my mother's every need. I was worried. She didn't look the same. She was pale. That brickhouse shape she once had was deflated. I stepped back and looked at the numbers on the door. Was I at the right house? I didn't want to believe that the woman who opened the door was my mother, but it was her and I was at the right house.

"How are you?" I asked Mama.

"Fine. Rachael is in town," she answered.

I followed Mama inside. She sat down on the couch and reached for her cup of tea. Andrea walked in and poured a fresh cup on top of the lukewarm tea. Rosie had the day off. She's Mama's bitch. They do not get along for shit, but Rosie takes good care of my mother. Rosie and Mama have a love/hate relationship. They claim they cannot stand one another, but you can feel and see the love between them. Andrea is calmer.

"Give me some vodka on ice, Darling. Thanks."

She didn't sound the same.

I sat across from Mama. "So…"

Mama sat back and crossed her legs. She pulled a pack of cigarettes from her purse.

"Did you see her?" she asked as Andrea lit her cigarette for her.

Mama inhaled then exhaled. She smiled and thanked Andrea. Andrea nodded and walked off. "She said she wanted to tell you about the baby."

"Excuse me?"

"She had a baby. Her name is Quandra. Rachael said you are the father," Mama said as she sipped the vodka.

I wanted to wrap my hands around her neck and squeeze.

"Mama, that is not my baby. I had no idea she was pregnant."

"She told me. She told me when she found out."

"Ma."

"Jaime, we can get a test."

"Ma, I cannot believe you kept this from me."

"If you are worried about her telling your wife, I told her not to because I knew it would hurt you. And I couldn't hurt my baby."

"So, you been playing Grandma to a baby that might not be mine?"

"You were so into that girl Ashanti. How could I even get close to you let alone tell you something so personal?"

I shook my head. I was disgusted.

"Ma."

"Spending my money."

"That's my money. She is my wife and I love her."

Mama laughed as she sipped her vodka.

"How much would she love you if she found out you had a baby by a woman she hates?" I stood up. "Don't fuck with me boy," she continued.

"I don't know you anymore. Stay away from me."

I had to tell my wife before someone else told her. I rushed home to see her. I opened the door and was face to face with my father. It looked as if he had seen a ghost.

"Hey, Man."

"Hey, Pops."

I tossed my keys into the crystal bowl by the door. I took off my leather jacket and tossed it on the couch. The fireplace was lit and two glasses of apple cider were on the coffee table.

"What are you doing here?"

"I can't come see my son?" he asked.

I walked over to him and hugged him. My father doesn't like to get in the middle of nonsense, and by the way he looked, he was not happy.

"So," we broke away from one another. "You know about Rachael's daughter?"

I nodded.

"Where is Ashanti?"

"She is in the bedroom. She came back to get a few things to take back to her mother's."

I needed to tell her before any of those snake in the grass mutha fuckers got to her. I pushed the bedroom door open. She was sitting on the edge of the bed. Her shoulders were low. I could tell she had been crying.

"Hey, Ashanti."

"Hey, Baby," she said as she turned towards me. Her eyes were bloodshot. She sniffled and asked, "What's up?"

"Nothing," I said as I sat on the edge of the bed and took her hand.

She placed her left hand on top of mine.

"You're shaking like a leaf. What's wrong, Love?" she asked me.

I calmly explained to my wife that I might have a seventeen-year-old daughter by Rachael.

"Excuse me?"

"Baby, it was one time. I swear."

She sniffled and asked, "How did you find out?"

"My mother."

Ashanti palmed her belly and asked me how I could do this to us. My heart shattered into a million pieces. I needed a drink. She cried uncontrollably but wouldn't let me get close to console her. She was shaking.

She stood up from the bed. The crying stopped. The next thing I knew, Ashanti grabbed the lamp from the nightstand and hauled it at me. I ducked. It missed my head by a feather. My father burst through the door and grabbed Ashanti. She was screaming in agony and pain, telling me to get out. She didn't want to see me anymore. Somehow, she broke away from my father, charged towards me like a bull, and told me to get out because she never wanted to see me again. Pops led me out of the bedroom.

"Here," Pops handed me a set of keys. "Go chill at my place."

I looked down at the keys. "Your place?" I asked.

Pops poured himself some vodka, took a long sip, and said, "I'm leaving your mother."

It felt like someone hit the back of my head with a hot sledgehammer.

"Pops."

"I can't take it. The lies. The hate. Look, I will get Altovise to pack you some things and bring them over tomorrow. You better get out of here. I hear her rumbling around back there."

"Thanks, Dad."

Pops texted the address as soon as I got in the car. This has been one messed up holiday. I wanted to be home eating turkey and mashed potatoes. Instead, I was running ragged.

♥

My father's place is laid out. I was impressed. The condo was a tad smaller than mine. Pops had wall to wall carpeting, leather furniture, and glass coffee tables. There is an awesome view of Federal Hill. The window extends around the entire condo.

"Ouch!"

I didn't feel no one creep up behind me. The person fucked my head up with the handle of a broom.

"Turn around with your hands up."

I knew it was Rosie. I turned around slowly, then snatched the broom from her and tossed it to the side.

"What are you doing here?" I asked her.

"I work here," she said.

"I'm going to crash here," I exhaled as I tossed my jacket on the couch. "You bouncing from house to house?" I asked as she nodded with her hands firmly placed on her hips. "First you were at my place and now you're here at Pop's place."

"I go where they tell me to go," Rosie responded.

"Can you check on Ashanti?"

"Sure. What happened?" Rosie asked.

"I honestly don't know."

Rosie and I sat on the couch.

"I thought you were going to New York."

Rosie closed her eyes and exhaled. "I am. Are you going to be okay, Love?"

I shook my head. "I have no idea."

"Well," Rosie jumped up from the couch, "let's do something I taught you how to do when you were six."

"Roll up?"

"Exactly. I got some Amsterdam in the fridge."

"Ok. Roll up."

Chapter Seventeen

LOVE HURTS

It was the day of the church's pre-"Thanks for Giving" choir rehearsal and dinner for selected less fortunate in the neighborhoods. Mama asked Jaime for two pans of his famous macaroni and cheese. Everybody loves it. But I don't care for it. He puts nothing but butter, milk, a ton of cheeses, seasoning, and love into it. I'm not saying that it's not good. We had a pan for our wedding, and it went. People came back for seconds and thirds. I just wasn't in the mood to eat anything.

Since I'd found out I was pregnant, everything was a turn off. Mother Lucille at the church makes the best strawberry pie. She makes it every holiday. Well, this holiday, I passed. She waltzed over to me with the pie in hand. It looked and smelled really good. I wasn't feeling it though. But since I didn't want anyone to know that I was pregnant, I took the pie and thanked her. She asked me if I was feeling well, and I told her that I was a little under the weather.

She smiled and said, "You look pregnant."

I laughed it off and shook my head no. Then, I smiled once more and walked away from her. The women in this church are very intrusive. They will get deep into your business.

Everyone was having a good time. I tried to have fun too, but I couldn't get into the holiday spirit. How could I? I had just walked out on the love of my life. There was no life or fun left in me.

Altovise was setting up chairs in the dining hall in the church basement trying her best to keep everything under control, but no one was listening to her. I stopped and asked her who told her she was in charge? We do this every year. I am sure everyone knows how to put chairs under the table and how many people sit at a table. We do not need anybody bossing us around. Sherri and her husband were slicing up desserts. Mama told me to keep an eye on them. Sherri's husband has really bad diabetes. He doesn't take his medicine and is always drinking and eating stuff he has no business drinking and eating.

I said, "Mama, that was real smart putting a really bad diabetic that does not take his medicine in charge of the sweets."

Elliott was upstairs tuning up the organ. Mama was running around like a chicken with its head cut off. She asked everybody in the dining hall fifty times if they had seen Elliott.

I laughed and said, "He's upstairs hiding."

Mama said he was supposed to help her make plates for the sick and shut in. I laughed. She asked me if I could go up there and get him. I shook my head no as I wrapped my shawl around my shoulders and joined Altovise in the kitchen. Elliott tuning up the instruments meant that he was not helping in the kitchen. And rightfully so. He is always helping out at the church. No one puts in more work than he does.

I went and hid with my sister in the kitchen with a huge cup of iced tea and lemon. Altovise was trying to convince me to go back home to Jaime. I told her that I would think about it. I didn't want to be pregnant and alone. I decided to get off my butt and enjoy the evening. As soon as I did that, Red and Felix entered the dining hall with four pans of macaroni and cheese. You would've thought Diddy himself walked in the way those church girls swooned over Red.

The elders in the church would die if they knew what he was down here doing and what his soul purpose was for trying to get these naïve Christian girls.

"What's up?" he asked.

I said, "Like you don't know. Don't be coming up in here making these church girls lose their train of thought."

Red laughed and shrugged as if he didn't know what was going on. My mother was acting like a damsel in distress. She asked Red and Felix could they stay and help serve the food. They said that wouldn't be a problem. Knowing Red, he probably had his eye on the biggest ass in the room and was trying to holla.

After Red set up in the dining hall, he made his way over to me. I shook my head, thinking, *Here he come trying to get on my good side. Probably want to know what's going on with me and Jaime.* Before I knew it, Red and I were wrapped in a warm embrace. He held on tight and long. I smiled. Once he finally let go, he escorted me over to the table. We talked about Rachael and his aunt. Red told me that Rachael was in town because her child was sick and she went to Mrs. Harris for help. I laughed.

Red was dead ass serious.

He said, "Yeah, she came to town about a week ago. The girl is pretty. She's supposed to be Jaime's."

I was hot. I wanted to kill my husband. Why after all this time did Rachael want to come and claim Jaime as Quandra's father? Was it because Quandra was seventeen years old and in need of a kidney? I needed to clear my head.

When Jaime finally showed up at the church acting like some big shot and donating money, I was done with him. There was no reason for him to be there. The damage between us was done and I was not in the mood for drama. He had broken my heart.

♥

Dinner was at 5:00 p.m. I was so excited to see my family. Mama laid out a beautiful spread. The wine was on chill and there was fresh turkey, cranberry sauce, stuffing, mashed potatoes and gravy, macaroni and cheese, sauerkraut and pig tails, fried fish, fried chicken, ham, sweet potatoes with marshmallows, ox tails, rice and peas, fried cabbage with ham, collard greens, cornbread, and hot buttered rolls.

After the celebration at the church, Altovise and I drove home to Mama's. When we pulled up in front of her house, I asked Altovise could we ride down to Jaime and I's place. I wanted to see him. He and I didn't get a chance to talk at the church and I needed to know more about the girl that was supposedly his. When we got there, I told Altovise to stay in the car while I went inside.

I unlocked the door to see Jaime's father sitting on the couch with his head in his hands. He had a bottle of vodka next to him. I walked over to the couch and gave him a hug. He asked how was everything. I broke the news and told him that I was pregnant.

He said, "That's wonderful, Ashanti, congratulations."

I thanked him and told him I was going into the bedroom to get a few items.

I got up from the couch and went into the bedroom hoping Jaime would be in there. I exhaled and shook my head. I should've known that he wasn't going to be here. I don't know why I set myself up for this nonsense.

I called Altovise and told her that I would be down in a few. Then, the bedroom door opened and Jaime came in and told me that there is a possibility Quandra might his daughter. I was so hurt. I couldn't believe what was happening. I was furious. I wanted to kill Jaime. Thank goodness his father burst through the door and held me back. Jaime Sr. tried to calm me down.

I knew it was a bad idea to come down here. Why did I come down here? I thought to myself.

I had a little hope that things were going to turn out different. I was wrong.

I didn't tell Altovise what happened. When we got back to Momma's house, I went straight to bed while everyone cooked. I'm usually up cooking and tasting with them until 3:00 a.m. I missed taste testing Mama's homemade stuffing. She makes the cornbread first. Altovise and I always have to have the first slice out of the pan. She made three pans from what I heard. Daddy got a fryer and fried a turkey. I didn't get any of it because I was fast asleep.

I was so sick the next day that I didn't see the Radio City Rockettes perform at the Macy's Thanksgiving Day parade. I laid in bed drinking tea and eating crackers, trying to keep the vomit down. I switched between the parade, *Elf*, and the new version of *The Little Rascals*. Altovise checked in on me between breaks. I even missed out on Mama's Thanksgiving omelets. Every Thanksgiving, Mama makes breakfast while making dinner. We eat, prep, and everyone catches up. I slept for most of the day, but I was determined to get up and eat something.

Mama was in the kitchen. I spoke to my family. I didn't tell anyone I was pregnant, but I was glowing. I couldn't wait to hold my little boy or girl. I rubbed my belly and whispered to the baby that we were with family and that this was our first Thanksgiving together. I never felt more alive yet alone.

"Love, want me to make you a plate?" Mama asked. I nodded as I made my way to the dining room table. Altovise and Tita were sitting next to one another with huge plates of food and tall glasses of wine. They reeked of weed.

Someone asked Mama to make a pot of coffee.

"Sure!" Mama yelled as she placed a plate of turkey, dressing, mashed potatoes, cranberry sauce, and sweets with marshmallow in front of me. I was happy when that plate came into view. I was hungry. I was also missing my husband.

I thanked my mother and father for hosting a wonderful evening. Mama asked if I was going home or staying another night. I told her I'd rather stay another night because I was so full from dinner that I couldn't move. I slept on the couch.

During the middle of the night, I caught a cramp in my side. One of the many joys of being pregnant. I rolled over on my left side and was face to face with my phone. I noticed that I had a few unread messages. They were all from Jaime. I exhaled and went back to sleep.

The next day, I had my first doctor's appointment. Altovise went with me for support. She stayed in the waiting area to talk on the phone and gossip with the staff. I had a sonogram done and they measured me to see exactly how far along I was.

"About time," Altovise said as I wobbled back into the waiting area.

She stood as I removed my Armani sunglasses from my forehead.

"When is your next appointment?"

"In six weeks."

"How was it?"

"Horrible," I laughed as we approached Altovise's Range Rover.

Altovise suggested that we should have a gender reveal party once we find out the sex of the baby, but I didn't want to be bothered with any unnecessary parties. I wanted to know right then and there what I was going to have so I could start on my nursery.

I took out my phone and dialed Jaime's number.

"Hello."

"Who is this?" Rosie asked. She is always drunk.

"Where is Jaime?"

"He's sitting right here."

"Okay," I laughed, "can I speak to him?"

"He's with the undertaker."

My heart dropped. Nobody had called and told me anything.

"Who died?" I asked. "His mama?"

Rosie laughed. "Don't we all wish. No, Pete."

"I'll be over."

I hopped in the passenger side of Altovise's truck.

"I didn't know Pete passed."

"It was all over the news," Altovise said nonchalantly.

I turned and looked over at my sister with my shoulders shrugged and my hands in the air. Really? She hadn't told me that Jaime's cousin had passed.

"Come on, let's get over there. I bet somebody made a chocolate cake," Altovise said as she laughed and put on her seatbelt.

The fact that my sister was making light of someone's death did not sit well with me. I don't know if it was because of the hormones or what, but I couldn't stand her.

"Put on your seatbelt, Darling," she said to me as if I were a child.

I fastened my seatbelt as she started the car.

As we were backing out, the car jerked and I hit my forehead on the dashboard.

"Shit!" Altovise put the car in park. "That mutha fucker was not looking where he was going." My head was pounding. I touched my forehead. Blood was gushing down my face.

Altovise looked over and said, "Oh shit. Stay still, don't move."

An older black guy and a young white woman walked over to the car and asked how we were. Altovise said that I was four months pregnant and her sciatic nerve was on fire. I may have been a little dizzy, but I know for a fact Altovise does not have sciatica.

We were both taken away in an ambulance. Altovise played her injury up to the hills. She was acting a damn fool and I was the one that was in extreme pain. Most importantly, I was thinking about my baby. I tried to keep calm, but my blood pressure was through the roof.

I was seen immediately. My back and head were hurting. My heart raced.

I kept asking the hospital staff, "Is my baby going to be okay?"

I didn't know what was going on. The doctor and nurses in the emergency room were speaking all at once and it sounded like gibberish. The baby was active. I tried to hold my stomach, but the nurse insisted that I remain calm and relax so that my blood pressure would go down.

I was stitched up, put on an IV drip, and given medication that wouldn't harm the baby.

The door to my hospital room opened and Jaime rushed in.

"Baby," he said while kissing my face, nose, ears, and stroking my hair. "I'm so sorry. How are you?"

"I'm okay," I said.

"Is the baby okay?" he asked, palming my belly.

I grabbed his hands and nodded. Tears rolled down the side of his face.

"Mama Bond called and told me. I'm so sorry," he said while hugging me tightly.

In that moment, I fell in love with him all over again.

The emergency room nurse finally came with my discharge papers. She said the baby and I were just fine, but I had to take it easy and get plenty of rest.

Jaime and I went to the waiting area of the emergency room to wait for the drama queen, Altovise. He grabbed a couple of waters from the vending machine, popped the tops, and gave me a bottle.

"Sorry about Pete."

He nodded. "He overdosed."

"Where is Felix?" I asked.

"I don't know, Baby," Jaime said as he shrugged and sipped his water.

I rested my head on Jaime's shoulder. As soon as I did, Altovise came out in a damn wheelchair. Jaime and I laughed.

"You really wanna go to Maui," I teased.

"Help me to the car," she whispered.

I cracked up.

"Shut up," she said.

"Altovise, I am not picking your big ass up," Jaime said.

We laughed.

"Come on. Let's go get something to eat. My treat," Jaime offered.

Altovise wheeled that chair out of the emergency room fast. I couldn't get out of there quickly enough; I was about to pee on myself from laughing.

Instead of going home, Jaime suggested that we go to Pete's to grab a bite to eat. That was a wonderful surprise. I was in the mood for something hot and spicy. Well, the baby was in the mood for something hot and spicy, so that's all I ate. I do not like spicy food. We walked into the restaurant and Rachael and Jordan were at the bar laughing, eating wings, and intentionally being loud, rude, and obnoxious. Altovise was pissed. She walked over and asked them what the fuck they were doing.

It took Van, Stephan, and Jaime to hold me back from going over to them to speak my mind. Jordan stood up to my sister and asked her what her mutha fucking problem was. All I remember is Nick hoping over the bar and holding my sister back.

"This man just lost his fucking family and you over here playing games. Let me the fuck go," Altovise screamed.

Gisselle stepped in and told Rachael and Jordan to leave. I don't know why they were there in the first place. Van said that he overheard Rachael telling Jordan that Jaime's mother gave her $500,000.00. Stephan shook his head, helped me into the back of the sweethearts bakery, then gave me some water and told me to calm down.

"It's going to be okay," he said.

I looked at my friend and broke down. It was all too much to handle. I needed a vacation.

Chapter Eighteen

NEVER CAN SAY GOODBYE

The days leading up to Pete's funeral were a disaster. The family was fighting over money. Pat, Pete's mom, said that there wasn't any money to split between the children because Pete did not have life insurance. Pat said she had insurance on him, but when he got married and had all those children and mistresses, she made his first wife the beneficiary, and whatever she did with the money is her business.

Jaime asked Pete's first wife if she had the policy. She told him she didn't know what he was talking about because she didn't have anything. Pat was furious.

Jaime said, "Forget about it. We have the money, let's bury my brother."

The morning of the funeral, I couldn't get myself together. I kept vomiting. Jaime woke up at 5:00 a.m., did his workout, then returned to the condo and made shrimp, fried fish filets, and grits. He brought a nice healthy plate to bed with toast, fruit, and coffee. I thought I was able to keep it down, nope. Five minutes after I ate, I had gut wrenching nausea, and all my breakfast came up.

Jaime said, "Damn, I might as well have poured everything down the damn toilet."

I said, "You should've."

I looked at the clock on the nightstand. It was time for us to get dressed. Then, I looked over at Jaime and caressed his back. He exhaled. I asked him if he was ready. He lowered his head and shook it no.

At the church, Pat finally made her way to the coffin to say one last goodbye to her only child, Peter Alexander. I could not stop crying. I cannot imagine outliving my child and looking down on him in a casket. Pat stretched her arms out wide, mumbled a prayer, leaned over the coffin, and cried. Pete's baby mama, girlfriend, wife, and a couple of mistresses were all there gossiping and throwing around rumors that Felix was there when Pete died. Everybody knows Felix does drugs. That's no secret, but they should have had some respect for the family. They are so tacky. It was a damn shame that even in death, Pete was talked about. I don't understand how a man like Pete fell into traps with those loose women. They were the worst bottom of the barrel women Baltimore had to offer. The kind you do not bring home to Mama.

Pete was such a sweetheart. He loved sex, drugs, fun, and he kept to himself most of the time. I don't know what went wrong.

I looked around the church. I didn't see Felix. Jaime said they were out using with the girls from the club when somebody must've given Pete some bad drugs. I cannot imagine him going out like that. Altovise said that he was with those nasty strippers from Big Daddy's. Those girls are nothing but trouble. Trashy ass girls with no morals. Hood. Ratchet. If I was a man, I wouldn't fuck them with a sick dick.

Altovise said Felix's low life ass was on the corner smoking weed with Red and Cletus. Cletus needs to get a damn job and take care of his fifty children. Altovise loves Cletus. Every time I try to say something about him, she gets mad at me. Altovise told Felix he was next. She said that Felix probably gave Pete that final shot in his damn arm. He was always jealous of Pete. We all knew that. Felix is also jealous of Jaime.

The story is that Pete, Felix, and Cletus had such a good time the night they went out with Jaime that they went out again the next night with one of the girls from the club named Carmelita.

She's the money maker at Big Daddy's. She's the reason, right along with her hood ass nasty ass stepmother, why they're open and can pay the rent.

Carmelita and Wes are friends. So, you know what was going down at that party. Carmelita does everything. She's pretty as a picture, sexy, and stops traffic. But the girl is dangerous. She sleeps with men and women. She introduced her husband, Chance, to some straight freak shit. They invited Jaime and I to an orgy once. We declined. They like to get down with whoever, whatever, and do anything. Carmelita's pussy and booty hole got serious mileage.

Chance used to work for a popular accounting firm. Now he is one of the financial backers and an accountant at Pete's. And believe me when I tell you, Jaime pays him excellent money. Chance is an older gentleman of refined taste and to be honest, he makes enough money for Carmelita not to dance. Chance was out of town when Carmelita hosted the hotel party where Pete was found dead. Carmelita called Chance and told him to come home because something bad had happened. Altovise said that Chance was in Atlanta with his pregnant twenty-one-year-old side piece.

Felix, Pete, and Red met up with Cletus. Felix said that he got a call from Carmelita saying that she was having this hotel party and when they got there, she was the only piece of pussy in the room. Red said he brought a box of condoms because Carmelita makes men cum in seconds. He also said that she's a dream come true and will let you do whatever you want to her. She don't ask for money; all she want to do is cum. Red said she jumped from one dick to the next dick and did not stop until she was satisfied.

Red said they were drinking and smoking and fucking and having a good ass time. He said that Carmelita was fucking everybody in the room. She didn't care because she was gone off Molly. Red don't roll Molly. He said that Pete was alive when they left. Red told him to come on, but Pete was busy getting his dick sucked by Carmelita in the bathroom. Red said Pete said that he wasn't leaving until he busted some nuts in her butt.

The next day, Aunt Patricia called asking Jaime where Pete was. He had not shown up to take her to work and he had her Lexus. Jaime called Red. Red said that when they left him, Pete was in the bathroom with Carmelita. Now we are burying Pete. No one claims to knows what happened. Pete was found in the alley with two needles stuck in his arms and his pants down. His wallet and credit cards were gone.

Carmelita said that one of the girls from the club, Destiny, came to the hotel. She said that Pete wanted her and Destiny to get down, but she had to go home.

I asked, "Go home for what?"

Carmelita is not going to leave no party with drugs, pussy, and dick until the drugs, pussy, and dick are gone.

Destiny lives a block over from where they found Pete. She could have looked out her window and seen the crime scene perfectly. No one has been arrested. They say no money was gone from his account. I don't understand.

Carmelita maintains her innocence. She said once her and Pete were done, she went to sleep, and when she woke up, Pete was still in the bathroom getting high. That's when Destiny showed up and starting freaking and snorting off in the bathroom with Pete. Carmelita said they were fucking.

She said she told them, "Check out is at 12:00 p.m. We have to go because I am not being charged extra."

She said that Pete said, "I'm coming. Go on. Do you have any more heroin?"

Carmelita said she told him, "No, but there's a dude in the next room with some good ass dope. Here's his number, call him."

She said she left after that.

I hate Cletus. He looks like a damn Cletus. His mother and father brought him from down south to Baltimore to start his life over. He got in more shit up here. Cletus stayed with Jaime and I for a week. He had to go. He took off his shoes and lit up the condo.

Jaime gave Cletus a job working at the restaurant under the table making $7.00 an hour. Cletus worked five days a week, then he got disability and food stamps. Jaime told me he gave his mother the stamps because she wasn't working. I admired him for that. He just needs to get his life together.

The whole situation with these so-called grown ass men and women surrounding Pete's death was uncalled for. Pete has no business being dead. But, he loved dope more than life itself, and it took his life. The detectives said anybody could've came and checked his wallet, took his phone, and kept it moving. It happened in the nastiest part of west Baltimore, with no camera footage. So, we are left with no answers. And who is going to investigate a damn junkie overdose in Baltimore? No one.

Jaime was shaking like a leaf getting ready to fall to the ground when he stepped up to the coffin and looked down at Pete. Pete was put away nice. He had on a blue suit, a black button-down dress shirt, and polished shoes. I held Jaime's hand. His cousin Mari tapped him on the shoulder. I turned. She whispered something in his ear. Jaime let go of my hand and dashed out of the church. His father and uncle were not too far behind him. Pat asked what was going on. I shrugged. I had no idea. Mari told Pat that they found Jaime's mother in the hall of the church unresponsive. I turned my head as if I did not hear a word.

After the service, I rode in the limo with Pat to the cemetery and back to her house for the repast catered by Pete's. I stayed with Pat the entire time while she talked to guests and gave out hugs and kisses. She didn't eat, and she looked thin and pale.

Later that night, we sat out on the porch. Rosie was there smoking a blunt. Pat asked what I was naming the baby. I told her Jaime. She smiled.

"Want some coffee, Honey?" Pat asked as she eased out of the chair. She looked pained.

"No thanks," I said as she caressed my shoulders as she passed. "I can't have caffeine."

"Okay, Love."

Rosie had disappeared. I don't know where she had gone. I closed my eyes for a hot second. When I opened them, I heard a crash. Pat had fallen while carrying a tray of coffee and pie. I hurried my pregnant ass over to her. She smiled and said she was fine. Clearly, she was not. I offered to help her clean up, but she declined. She told me to go home and get some rest. Rosie offered to drive me.

I hadn't heard from Jaime in hours and I was wondering what was going on. To my surprise, he was home at the kitchen counter listening to Earth, Wind & Fire, smoking a blunt, and drinking scotch. His shoulders slouched.

"Hey," I said as I tossed my keys into the crystal bowl by the front door. "I haven't seen you in forever."

He nodded as he took another puff on the blunt and said, "Stress."

We chuckled.

"No shit," I responded. "Wanna do a spa day tomorrow, just the two of us?"

"My mother is dying."

"Jaime," I said as I sat next to him, "drinking is not going to take the pain away."

I caressed his shoulders. He exhaled and moved back. I exhaled.

"I don't want you to go out like that," I said. "Alcohol is not a problem solver. I don't want to lose you to drinking."

Jaime took another swig of scotch and asked, "Can you please leave me alone?"

"No."

"Ashanti," he cried out with tears in his eyes, "let me deal!"

"If you need me..."

Tears fell from his face like a waterfall, "I know where to find you."

I went into the bedroom, closed the door, and left my husband to his pain.

♥

Jaime's mother passed a week before Christmas. I wish we could've celebrated the holiday, but instead we were mourning the loss of Jaime's mother.

I thought the passing of his mother would bring us closer together, but nope.

Chapter Nineteen

SHAMELESS

I wasn't ready to give up on my marriage just yet. I wanted to give it one more try. I love Jaime. He is the love of my life. I don't know where I would be without him. I was sitting at the kitchen counter having a cup of warm chai tea, a buttered croissant, and some fruit when he finally woke up. Jaime bakes croissants and freezes them in individual freezer bags. Whenever I want one, I grab it and stick it in the toaster oven. They taste just like they came fresh from the oven.

Jaime went straight to the coffee and made himself a cup. He leaned on the counter and snatched an orange slice from my plate. I smiled as I stood up.

"How are you feeling?" I asked as I carefully placed the plate in the sink. "You slept like a log. I had to sleep on the couch."

He laughed as he turned to the stove.

"Hungry?" he asked as he gathered pans.

I shrugged.

"When is your next doctor's appointment?"

I was surprised that Jaime was up as much as he drank last night. I entertained him.

"Not sure," I responded. "What are you making?"

Jaime exhaled as he walked over to the fridge.

"Eggs, bacon, and pancakes."

"Oh, well, I'm kind of full."

"Please."

I paused.

"Sure, Love," I responded. "Let me go get my phone."

"No," he pleaded. "No phone. Just me, you, and breakfast. I want to talk to you."

I smiled and whispered, "Sure."

I sat down at the counter slowly and watched as he grabbed the eggs, a glass bowl, salt, and pepper.

"Scrambled?"

I nodded as he cracked six eggs into the glass bowl and stirred.

"Cheese?"

"Of course. What we got?"

Jaime headed over to the fridge and checked.

"American, provolone, cheddar," he said then stood with the fridge door open while waiting for me to make a choice.

"Cheddar."

Jaime snatched the cheddar from the fridge.

"Mama's funeral is next week. I'm waiting for people to get in."

"Have you been to the house?" I asked while watching as he turned on the stovetop then placed the eggs to the side and started on the bacon.

"Which one?" he giggled. "She has three."

He paused.

"Not yet," he continued. "I'm not ready."

He paused again then turned to me.

"Look, I wanted to tell you about Quandra."

My heart dropped. I wasn't ready for the conversation but it needed to be had.

"I just found out myself. I don't even know if she is mine, Ashanti. Believe me. You are the only woman I ever loved."

"I believe you."

"Everything just happening so fast. I'm the type of guy that takes control of things but as of lately, Baby, I feel like I am losing my shit."

He returned to the stove to finish cooking breakfast.

"So, how much time are you taking off after the baby is born?" I asked him.

"I can finally see myself taking time off, after hiring Mila. She hired a full staff. I am so happy. It's taking a lot of stress off me."

"So, that means you will be there to witness the birth of your son?"

"Absolutely," he said then asked me, "How many pancakes would you like?"

"Three."

"You got it. Blueberry?"

"You know it."

♥

It was the morning of the funeral. I was so sick. Jaime drank a bottle of Hennessy every night and cried himself to sleep. I told him that he needed to stop drinking, but who I am to tell a grieving man what to do? His drinking was getting out of control. I told his father, but he only made matters worse by encouraging the drinking.

There were so many cars heading towards the church. Pat, Jaime, and I were in the first limo behind the hearse. Pat was in good spirits, but Jaime was a shaking wreck. There was a line leading into the church. They had to open the line up so the family could enter. I never knew a woman so evil could have such a good turnout for her funeral. But like Mama said, they were really there for Jaime.

It was a funeral fit for a queen.

Jaime's mother was laid to rest in a white, satin coffin. She wore a purple dress, diamond earrings, a diamond tennis bracelet, and white gloves. In the days leading up to her death, she wasn't pleasant on the eyes. But, today, she looked impeccable and at peace. She looked like herself.

Jaime, Pat, and I walked into the church together. I had to sit down. My feet hurt and they looked like rolls of fresh dough. I sat down on the first row of pews and slid out of my shoes. This baby was making my life a living hell.

A crowd of people came to give everyone on the front row hugs. I was obviously pregnant, so everyone congratulated us. I sat there rubbing Jaime's back. By the time the service started, I was numb. Pat kept leaning over and making light of the day. She said her stomach was growling.

I leaned back and said, "I know, I heard it."

She laughed and we held hands.

The line of mourners entering the church was slowing down. Out of the corner of my eye, I saw a tall, slender chick dressed in all black with a pretty girl by her side. The girl looked like she was a teenager. Everybody in the sanctuary wondered who they were, and the teenager looked confused too. Jaime had his head in his hands.

"I can't believe Rachael and Quandra showed up," Pat whispered.

I turned to study Quandra. She was a thin, very pretty, chocolate girl with big brown eyes and long black hair down to her ass. But, she looked nothing like Jaime.

I thought to myself, *Rachael had better go and find who her baby father is because it is not my husband.*

After the service, the sun was shining bright, the sky was a beautiful blue hue, the birds were singing, and there was a cool breeze blowing. As Jaime and I leaned against the limo outside of the church, he told me to go home and rest. It had been a very long day and an extremely long funeral service. I just wanted to go home, soak, and take a nap.

Jaime told me to take the limo home and he would meet me there. I asked him how he was going to get to the cemetery. He said that it was behind the church. I hadn't noticed. I jumped into the limo, kissed his beautiful lips, and went home.

The ride to the condo was smooth. I drank a bottle of water and snacked on cashews. I love cashews, but they have to be Planters fancy whole cashews or nothing at all. I was happy that the funeral was over. It felt like the weight of the world was off my shoulders. I know Jaime felt better because he looked better after the service.

Rachael and Quandra never made their way over to Jaime. I wondered if she made her move when I left, but I will never know. I never asked and he never spoke of it. The fact that the issue of Jaime's past infidelities, his drinking, and Rachael being back in the picture was ruining everything did not sit well with me.

Chapter Twenty

LOVE'S IN NEED

"Jaime!" Monica yelled over the crashing of the pans and the noise in the kitchen.

I came to work to ease my mind. I had been in the kitchen since 7:00 a.m. and I was ready to go the hell home. I ran a crab cake and barbeque rib special with two sides and a piece of chocolate cake. My mother loved my chocolate cake.

"Yeah," I answered her as she walked into the kitchen with a tray full of dirty dishes.

She walked to the dishwasher and handed them to Felix. Sweat was pouring from my forehead as I called for Alexis to come and get her table plates.

Monica walked up next to me, took my towel from my waist, and swiped the sweat from my face. I smiled and thanked her.

"Belle is sick."

"What's wrong with her?' I asked as I reached for a plate of crab cakes. I looked at the ticket and added potato salad and green beans to the order. Then, I looked inside the potato salad tin and saw that it was now empty.

"Red, I need more potato salad online, please."

Monica shrugged her shoulders.

"She said she's going home. She said if you want, she can come back tonight."

I shook my head no and told Monica to tell Belle not to worry about coming back in. I reminded Monica that Van and Brendan were coming in at 2:00 p.m. and Chance was coming in at 4:00 p.m. We didn't need Belle to come back. Monica nodded as she pulled her cell phone from her apron and walked out of the kitchen. I hope she was calling Belle because my hands were full.

Tickets were coming in faster than we could keep up. I called for Monica and asked her what kind of wait we were on. Judging by the tickets coming in, we needed to be on at least a two-hour wait. She came back into the kitchen with her cell phone plastered to her ear. She told me that we were on a one-hour wait. I demanded that they up the wait and not sit anymore customers until we got the current tickets in. My servers were coming into the kitchen asking me what was going on, but I had no idea. I stepped off the line and asked Alexis to expedite until I got back. I washed my hands in the small sink and went downstairs. There was a line out the door.

Gisselle and Swazzette were at the host stand. I asked them what was going on. Gisselle said that Swazzette misjudged and kept seating people in the bar and putting people on a one-hour wait. I checked the wait list and shook my head.

I stepped in and said, "We are not seating any more people until dinner."

"What about the people that are waiting?" Gisselle asked.

Did she really just ask that stupid ass question? I tried not to let my frustration show. My cell phone was blowing up. Why are they doing this to me while I am trying to stay calm?

"Let them know that it's a two and a half hour wait," I said as I stepped behind the podium while respectfully asking Swazzette to step aside.

I pulled up the iPad and told her that the fifth patron down to the fifteenth needed to know that there was a two and a half hour wait. I had to give them a quick lesson on table turnover and let them know that by the time we got to the fifteenth patron on the waiting list, lunch was going to be over. Swazzette took in everything. Gisselle acted as if she had an attitude with me. I asked her what was wrong. She had the nerve to say that I was treating her like she doesn't know what she is doing.

I stepped back, snickered, then responded, "Obviously, you don't."

She had the gall to say that we didn't know what we were doing in the kitchen. I had to turn around to see who she was talking to. Swazzette held her lips in tightly. She didn't want anything to do with this. I don't blame her. I told Gisselle to go home. She exhaled, grabbed her purse, and left. I made an announcement to the patrons in the lobby, apologizing for the wait and offering a free app to whoever decided to stay. I had plenty of buffalo wings and mozzarella sticks I had to get rid of before the sell by date. Most of the patrons in the lobby didn't mind. They said they would be more than welcome to stay and wait. I told Swazzette that I was going to send Monica down to help out between tables. She apologized and said that Gisselle was the one that kept taking people and telling them there was a half hour wait.

I said, "I know. She thinks she owns this place. Ashanti is not in because the pregnancy was kicking her ass, but I had to remind Gisselle nicely, once again, who the boss is. Today, I had all that I could take from her. That backup was horrific. But, we can handle anything that is tossed at us."

"Yeah." Swazzette cheered.

I went back upstairs to the kitchen. Belle called and said that she got Monica's message and she would be in on Friday. I told her that if she needed more time off, she was more than welcome to take it because I was going to put these young people to work. Once I got off the phone with her, I made my way back to the line and told Monica to go and help Swazzette because I had sent Gisselle home. Monica held her mouth and cracked up. I asked her what was so damn funny.

She said, "You know exactly why I am laughing."

When Van and Stephan jumped online, it was going on 2:30 p.m. I told Stephan to offer free apps for the remainder of the day. Stephan always had a pen and paper in hand to write down important notes. I filled them in on the two-hour wait fiasco and sending Gisselle home. Van and Stephan laughed. I just shook my head and went to take a rest in my office.

I sat behind the desk, reached inside the drawer, and grabbed my half bottle of Hennessey. At first, I was going to make some wings with it, but I decided to have a drink instead.

"Jay," Juan knocked and came into my office without asking if he could.

"Yo," I said as I stood up and shook his hand.

"Can I get a hit of that?" he asked.

I nodded as I grabbed a paper cup from the desk and gave him a shot.

"What's up?" I asked him.

"Summer is mad at me."

I laughed as I took another shot. I told them young cats about fucking with those pretty ass girls they hire. Juan was messing around with this fine chocolate honey named Summer. She looks like she could be related to me. Her skin is flawless. She is a beautiful girl with a round ass and thick thighs. She looks like she breaks hearts and rides a mean ass dick. I told him not to deal with her, but he had caught feelings for that young ass girl. I love Summer's older sister, Lavender. Lavender worked at the club with Carmelita. I hooked Lavender up with a van for her and her children. I wanted to reach out to her, but I had all I could take with Carmelita. I was done with her before Pete passed, but I was really finished when she was the last one that saw him alive and had no clue as to what happened.

I know my cousin was an addict. It was something about those drugs that he could not shake. I named this restaurant after him to give him some kind of hope. He didn't have to work another day in his life. He could've come to work with us and kicked it. I think he got a hold of some bad drugs or just took too much, and his heart went out on him. I miss my cousin.

After I got off work, I went to the cemetery to pay my respects. I like to go out there and clear my head. I know Pete is not with us in the physical, but I had to let him know that Mama was gone and when she walks through the gates to take care of her until I get there.

I laughed out loud and said to myself, "If I do not stop drinking, it might be sooner than later."

I placed the bottle of Hennessey on Pete's grave. I told him that I loved him, and I would see him again.

I made my way to my father's house and had dinner with him. I told him that I was tired of fighting a losing battle. I wanted my wife and life back. It felt like I was in the twilight zone. My father was very comforting. He said that everything was going to be okay. I believed him.

Chapter Twenty-One

I LOVE YOU, BABY

The days leading up to my mother's funeral were heart-breaking. It felt like somebody hit me in the head with a sledgehammer. I had a headache for seven days straight. I called family and paid for most of them to come into town. Then I had to put them up in hotels because I didn't have room at the condo. I didn't mind though. You only get one mother and I wanted my family to be comfortable. My wife was by my side the entire time. She is a dream come true. I didn't think she would be there for me. After all the craziness my mother put her through, I thought she was going to skip out on everything.

The night my mother passed, I went home and cried like a baby. It felt like I had lost my mind. I never knew hurt until I watched her take her last breath. I wish she would've changed or made peace with Ashanti, but she was evil until the very end. I didn't think she could be, but she was horrible. I even asked her what was really going on. She said nothing.

My drinking was out of control. I had to drink before bed just to be able to stop crying and close my eyes to rest. I woke up in the middle of the night crying. I was standing in front of the undertaker crying. Everybody was there for me, but I felt alone. Scotch was my best friend.

The day before the funeral, Ashanti's aunts and mother made dinner for the viewing. I appreciated that. Everyone met up at Belle's house, ate, prayed, and then headed over to the funeral home for the viewing.

Before everyone else entered, I stepped inside the funeral home where my mother laid. A wave of cold air ran over me. I shuddered. I inhaled slowly then exhaled through my nose. This was it. I was saying goodbye to the love of my life one final time. I stood over her body and smiled. For the first time ever, she looked peaceful. I kissed her forehead and asked the undertaker if I could spray a little Chanel on her clothes so I could smell her once more. She nodded. I sprayed a little on her collar and placed the bottle in her coffin. I never wanted to smell Chanel again and since that day I haven't.

The family entered the sanctuary. I disappeared to my car with Tita and Altovise. Elliott joined us then we got messed up. We rolled up a fat blunt. We laughed and cried and laughed until Elliott threw up, then we laughed at that.

There was a light tap at the window. I was on the passenger side. Altovise was in the driver's seat, Tita and Elliott were in the back.

Altovise rolled down the window and a gush of smoke hit Ashanti in the face. She coughed. We laughed at that.

Ashanti leaned into the car and fanned smoke, "What in the hell are you fiends doing?" She stepped back. "Aunt Pat is looking for you."

I got out of the car. Altovise rolled up the window and laughed with Tita and Elliott about Ashanti being a party pooper.

I walked close to my wife and opened my mouth.

"Smell my breath," I said as I blew into her face.

She blinked twice and stepped back. Then she reached into her pocket, pulled out some mints, and placed one on my tongue.

"Chew," she smiled. "There you go."

I kissed her lips and asked was it that bad; she said it was worse.

Ashanti and I stood next to one another greeting and talking to guests. I handled the viewing better than I thought I would. I am so glad that Ashanti didn't leave.

After everyone left, Ashanti, Pops, and I stayed an extra fifteen minutes. Then Ashanti left, leaving Pops and I to cry together.

Tomorrow, I thought, *is going to be a bad day*.

The family came to the condo afterwards for dessert and coffee. I don't know who invited all them people. Altovise set up the kitchen with all kinds of cakes and pies and cookies on silver trays with pots of coffee, tea, and water. It was nice. It was the first time Altovise ever helped. That made me laugh.

I didn't want to be bothered with anyone. I grabbed a bottle of Hennessy and told Chuck to meet me on the patio.

"I spoke to the lawyer. You and Ashanti are going to have to go to physical therapy," Chuck told his wife. I chuckled.

Altovise's head was bobbing back and forth like one of those bobble heads.

"How am I going to fake something I don't have?" she asked as she poured more Hennessy into her cup. "I don't have sciatica."

It was a nice night out; it wasn't cold but it wasn't warm. In fact, it was unusually nice for December. I enjoy the cool weather. There were too many people inside. Ashanti had the faux fireplace on.

Altovise sipped slowly on her Hennessy then asked, "Don't you know some thug therapist that wants to come up?" She tried to stand. "Let me go see if Katrina knows somebody."

Katrina is my hood ass cousin. Nine times out of ten she knows someone that knows someone that is a "thug therapist" as Altovise put it.

"Y'all know some fucked up ass people," Altovise said as she walked away.

Chuck and I watched as she managed to stumble over to Katrina. Katrina was also fucked up. I don't know how that conversation went down but it was probably stupid.

I laughed and said, "Your wife is crazy."

Chuck slowly nodded in agreement as he poured more Hennessy into our cups. I drank mine straight with a little water on the side.

"How you deal?" I asked him.

"Drinking," Chuck laughed.

"Want another drink?"

"Yeah, I was wondering why you was beating around the bush. I want something to knock my socks off. I been drinking Hennessy since I was twelve. This is like drinking water," he said.

I agreed with him. I drank so much Hennessy it was weak to me too. Now, it might knock your socks off, but I've been drinking it with Rosie since I was eleven. I drank so much alcohol with that woman and her daughters. I slept with both of her daughters too. The pussy wasn't that good, but it wasn't bad. It was good enough to get a drunk nut off. I couldn't imagine running back and forth to that. One of them had some amazing head skills though. I don't remember which one but thinking about it almost brought me to tears. Or was it the Hennessy? Who knows.

"Follow me," I said.

I led Chuck down to the wine cellar that I share with three other people in the complex. I rarely see anyone down there. All three units are individually locked and have different entrances. My shit stay locked. I got nothing but the best down there. I even got some Louie XIII down there that my mother gave me as a wedding present.

I reached for the scotch on a rack high above our heads and handed it to Chuck.

"How old is this?" he asked

"Twenty," I responded with pride.

Chuck and I pulled up two crates, popped open the drink, poured a little, sipped, and nodded. That hit the spot.

I have cigars in the cellar as well. I grabbed two and handed one to Chuck. He bit the tip and lit it.

"I saw Rachael earlier," he said as he exhaled smoke through his nose. "She looking good."

"Yeah, Man, I know. She begging me to give her the d. I can't."

"You. Are. A. Good. Man," Chuck said.

He always said that Rachael was a beautiful woman. And although he never stepped out on Altovise (that's what he tells us), he said he would've given Rachael the business.

"I love my wife," I shrugged. "Rachael still calls once a day and she shows up at my job."

"After all these years?"

"I told her Ashanti and I are not divorcing, we are just spending time apart. That's my mutha fucking wife. We still fucking every day. I still pay all the bills. She carrying my child. I am going to take care of her until the day I die."

"I feel you."

"Even if she marries another man, I am going to take care of her. Rachael was a tight piece of ass back in the day though."

"I heard Rachael was the best in town. I was fucking her sister-in-law, Michelle," Chuck said.

I remember that. Between Monica's mother and Altovise, Chuck fucked with Michelle. It wasn't serious because he said he always had a thang for Altovise. Michelle was crushed when Chuck broke it off with her. Funny, as soon as he broke it off, she ended up pregnant. I asked Chuck was that his baby. He said no. My wife said she saw Michelle with a little girl that looks like Chuck. I don't know man; I just don't know about that. Michelle never said the baby was Chuck's. That was way over twenty years ago. I am sure Michelle does not care who her baby's daddy is. She has since married twice and is widowed with three children. One of the boys went to the NBA.

"I only fucked Rachael once and I swear I put it in her ass."

We laughed.

"Seriously, she's a freak. She got some good ass head."

Chuck nodded as he shook the ashes from his cigar.

"Best in town I heard."

"Dude, I was blown. Now she putting her oldest on me. I thought that was Crunchy baby for real."

Chuck said, "That dead mutha fucker. He got kids all over the fucking city. His funeral was filled with a bunch of ugly ass mutha fuckers like himself. They were crying and shit like they were going to miss him."

I laughed and added, "He died owing them money, that's why they were crying."

"Johanna, his sister, nice ass."

"Right."

"Where she get that from? The mama flat as an iron-ing board."

"I think she bought it."

Chuck and I laughed louder and clinked cups.

"To be honest, Rachael does not know who that baby's father is."

Chuck raised his cup and said, "I'll drink to that." As soon as my head hit the pillow that night, I fell asleep. I woke up at 7:00 a.m. then ran five miles on the treadmill. I was still tense so I made love to my wife. That made me feel better. I released so much stress out on my wife that if she wasn't pregnant, she would've been.

I took a long, hot shower then got dressed and made pancakes and bacon for Ashanti and myself. We sat and ate until it was time to go to the church.

I didn't want to get a limo, but my aunts and cousins said I should.

It was time to bury my mother. We arrived at the church. I asked all of my family to wear white. She was a mean ass woman, but she was regal. I loved her so much. I am going to miss her mean ass.

Ashanti held onto me. She was shaking. She does not do good at funerals. Who does? I had a drink before we got out of the limo. I told her to sip some. She laughed.

I whispered in my wife's ear, "Your big ass fall, I am not picking you up."

She laughed out loud. We led the procession. I stepped up to the coffin. I didn't look inside. Instead, I turned my head to the left. I exhaled as we walked back to our seats. Ashanti's hat was so damn big, on top of that big ass belly.

"Baby, that hat. You're not the First Lady."

"I'm your First Lady."

"I just want this to be over."

"Me too, Baby," she said. "Me too."

Rachael, Quandra, and Jordan stepped up to the coffin. Oh boy. Ashanti held on to me tightly. Rachael and Jordan walked past us and did not speak. I wasn't surprised at Rachael but Jordan?

How are you going to walk past Ashanti like she does not exist? See how people so quick to forget. My wife and Jordan were so close. Rachael done filled her head with lies. Jordan is weak minded. Anybody can play on her emotions, quick. I was sick of it. I hope I never see Rachael's troublemaking ass ever again. That troublemaking whore got some good ass head though. Damn shame all that talent's wasted.

Chapter Twenty-Two

MY BABY AND ME

Our anniversary is May 31. My due date was June 13. Jaime was busy opening another Pete's. He didn't go over anything with me. I had come home and there were two big, black dudes in nice suits and shined shoes with shiny cuff links and pinky rings at the table smoking Cuban cigars and drinking Louis XIII. The smoke was thick. Laughter was deep in the air. Jaime didn't introduce me to either of the men. I waved and Jaime blew a kiss and continued with the conversation.

I didn't know the reason behind the meeting with those men, but it did concern me a little. I had rushed to the bathroom and by the time I returned to the dining area, they were gone.

Jaime mentioned opening another Pete's in west Baltimore. I asked him if those dudes were going to run it. He smiled and said no. He said they were his father's friends.

I never imagined Jaime would open another Pete's, let alone so soon. It was literally the day after those men left that he was in negotiations with the landlord of our Owings Mills location.

Jaime was becoming the man in this town. He hired a PR team for the business. Anybody that wanted to get in contact with him had to go through his PR team, assistant, or management.

There was a huge groundbreaking ceremony in Owings. It brought out all of the local news media outlets. People were excited. Not only was this going to be a milestone in Jaime's life, but it was going to bring jobs to Baltimore. It seemed like he had an interview every week. He couldn't keep up with appearances. I know I couldn't. I was fat and pregnant.

Jaime said that he had received overwhelming responses from his four locations, so why not open another one on the west side of town? The real shock was the Pete's carry out on York Road. I never imagined that place would do the business that it does. I don't know anyone that deals in real estate on that side of town. All I know is that Jaime made a few phone calls and signed the lease without consulting anyone.

Once everything was taken care of, Jaime called an emergency meeting with his managers, assistants, and trainers. It was four or five years after he opened the Inner Harbor Pete's. He called us in at midnight. It was cold, raining, and water was rising in the Harbor. Security told us that they were keeping an eye on the water level and if it got bad we would have to leave. The "perks" of having a restaurant on the water.

There was tons of food on three tables in the bar area. Jaime told everyone to get a plate, sample everything, and be honest. There was sausage with grits and fried potatoes with cheese, bell peppers, and onions. Pancakes. Turkey bacon. Half and half. Club sandwiches. Subs. Pizza. You name it. That pizza was so good, we told him to put it on the menu at the Inner Harbor location.

Pete's York Road is reasonable. It's a simple carry out with chairs, restrooms, a grill, and there's about three people per shift--a cashier, a shift leader, and the cook. Our peak times are 10:00 a.m. to 4:00 p.m. When the kids get out of school, it's a wrap. They get off that number eight bus, come inside, and it turns into a madhouse. I've never worked there because I'm so busy with Inner Harbor, but Monica and all the girls went there to train Felix and Nick the bartender. They love it there. The York Road location closes at 6:00 p.m. After that time, you don't want to be in that part of town without police protection. Heck, you don't even want to be there in the daytime without police protection, but you gotta pick your battles.

We sat down with Belle, Monica, Gisselle, and Red to go over the menu and cost.

I said, "Baby there is already a popular carry out on York Road--Pop Daniel."

I grew up eating Pop Daniel. My mother went to school with Pop Daniel. Pop Daniel's grandfather used to go crabbing with my grandfather and they made crab cakes that knocked your socks off. Jaime's crab cakes are awesome, but Pop's is out of this world.

Pop Daniel Soul Food is banging. I felt guilty talking about Pop Daniel. Pop Daniel is Nick's father. I remember going there when Nick was cleaning tables and taking orders.

Jaime said, "He don't mind a little competition."

I was skeptical but, once again, I was going to stand by my man.

"I mean like…" Monica interrupted.

There was a bad ass thunderstorm going on. The lights blinked. I saw the security guard, Strauss, standing by the door and keeping an eye on the weather. I was scared. The thunder shook the building.

"Pop Daniel is popping," Monica continued.

I looked at Jaime and agreed with Monica. Pop D got it on lock.

"He got the other half of York Road sewed up. He banging, Jaime," she added.

Silence fell over the room.

"Let's do it. I mean, let the people decide," I said.

Everyone looked at me.

I continued on, "Let's do it. You do have the option of signing a six-month lease. Some people sign month to month leases. If it does good in the first six months, you know you got it. If not, we close. It's as simple as that, right?"

I exhaled as I looked over at my husband. He nodded then jumped up from the table.

"Let's do it. Nothing beats a fail but a try, right?" he said.

We knew it was going to be a lot of hard work. And it was going to be extremely hard on me since I was close to my due date. It meant that the baby and I were not going to see Jaime as much, but that's okay. I know what it took for him to get to this, and I was going to stand beside him one hundred percent. I have faith in him. I know his strengths and his weaknesses.

I am not going to lie to you, I had no idea that the Pete's York Road location was going to take off the way it did. It has been featured on various cable food channel shows, and both local and cable news outlets have been flocking to us. We are blessed.

Jaime has been to New York to be a judge on the popular Food Network show *Chopped*. I couldn't go. He flew up, did the show, and came right back. They asked him if he would like to come back and sit on the panel again in the future.

Everything was going well with us. We weren't living together but we were together. Jaime preferred it that way. Lord knows I did not. I wanted to go away for our anniversary, but Jaime wanted to stay home since I was about to pop. I was so big I could not see my feet. Jaime had to dry and lotion them after I showered. I felt helpless but good. I liked being pregnant, but towards the end, I didn't do anything so I felt helpless.

My baby shower was the first Saturday in June. I didn't lift a finger. My sisters handled everything from the food to the venue to the guest list. All I had to do was show up. I didn't want a big, extravagant baby shower. Believe it or not, I wanted a plain one.

The night before the baby shower, I went to bed early. I had been cramping all afternoon, but I wasn't alarmed cause I knew it was those dreaded Braxton Hicks contractions I'd heard about.

I propped a few pillows up on the bed, Jaime rubbed my feet and massaged my shoulders, and before long I was out.

I enjoyed myself at the shower. I had a jungle theme with a four-tier cake that had Jaime III name on it. I cried when I saw it. My sisters are jerks. They took tons of pictures while I was crying and posted them on social media. Jaime made all of the food. Just like at our wedding, he had to take over in the kitchen. We had shrimp, crab, lobster and lobster Alfredo, salad, mini cheesecakes, mimosas, fruit, apple juice, and coffee.

The shower was going to be buffet style, but somehow it ended up with servers and they brought our plentiful plates to our tables.

I ate a lot of cake and ice cream. I thanked my sisters for throwing me a lovely shower. It was one of the best showers I had ever been to.

Jaime packed up the Range with our gifts and he held my hand as he drove me home. I knew our relationship was getting better. When we got to the condo, he put all of the gifts in the baby's room. It was getting late, so he decided to spend the night and we went to bed.

I tossed and turned for a little bit then I woke up. When the pains let up, I went right back to sleep.

"Ooooooo!!!!!" I screamed as I was awakened by what felt like someone kicking me in the uterus.

Jaime sat up in the bed like Jason in those *Friday the 13th* movies. He took my hand in his and asked me what was wrong. I told him I was having contractions.

He leaned over, turned on the lights, and asked me if I was sure. Then, he palmed my belly. And just like that, the pain went away. I sat up, balanced myself on my elbow, and told him that was weird.

Jaime eased out of bed and went to use the bathroom. I eased out of the bed and wobbled into the bathroom behind him. He was standing at the sink washing his hands.

"Della Williams called," I told him.

Jaime let out a long sigh and turned off the water. He bit his bottom lip.

"I know," he said as he nodded, turned off the bathroom light, and headed back into the bedroom.

He climbed into bed. I stood in the archway of the bathroom.

"I talked to her," he continued.

I shrugged, "Okay."

He was not trying to tell me much about the conversation.

"She is retiring and wants to sell Della's."

"How much?"

Jaime shrugged, shook his head, and said, "I don't know. I have to make a few phone calls. You know the drill."

"So, you're buying a restaurant on top of opening another restaurant and your son is coming?"

"Yes. Why not?"

"Jaime, you're never here. Opening a new spot and buying a new spot means you're never ever going to be here."

"Baby, that's what employees are for."

"I thought you were going to open Owings Mills. You have the York Road carry out location, Annapolis, Harbor, and Towson. They are doing exceptionally well. I never see you."

"Ashanti, come on."

"I thought you said…"

"I know I said I wasn't doing anything until after the baby was born. But, he's not trying to come out."

We looked at one another and laughed.

"Give him time," I said. "I'm hungry."

"Me too."

"Want some pancakes?"

"You cooking?"

"Yup."

"You can't cook. The only thing you can do for me is be my wife. Stay in your lane," Jaime said.

"Really?!"

"Ashanti, Baby, I will never lie to you."

He pissed me off so I grabbed my body pillow and smacked the shit out of him.

He laughed and said, "I'm going to take a shower."

As I sat on the edge of the bed, Jaime eased out of it, went into the bathroom, and hopped into the shower. Just then, my phone rang but I couldn't find it. I hate that. As soon as mine stopped ringing, Jaime's rang. I reached for his, put in the passcode, and answered. It was my brother. It was weird for him to be calling in the middle of the night.

"Hey, Elliott. What's up, Love?"

Jaime stepped out of the bathroom with his towel wrapped around his waist.

"What's wrong?" he asked as he rubbed my back. Then he palmed my belly and asked if it was the baby.

I sat with hunched shoulders listening to my brother talk about how his boyfriend had dumped him. Jaime rubbed his head. Then, he reached for his phone and talked to Elliott. I couldn't talk. Instead, I rolled over onto my side of the bed, grabbed Jaime's pillow, and tried to go back to sleep. Then, cramps kicked in. I grabbed my pillow and placed it between my legs. It helped very little, but I was able to go to sleep.

Around 12:30 p.m., I woke up hungry and still cramping. I ate tuna fish and kale chips.

My phone rang all afternoon, but I didn't answer. As I was getting out of the shower, Jaime called and asked what I was doing. I told him I was getting dressed so I could hop in the Range, go to Popeyes, and see Mama. I couldn't sit in the house not doing anything. He told me to call him as soon as I got there.

I wasn't expecting a lot of people to be at Mama's house when I arrived, but there were so many cars parked out front that I had to park behind the house.

Mama was at the kitchen table with the house phone next to her.

"Hey, Mama," I said as I gave her a big hug and kiss.

Mama had a box of tissue in front of her and her coffee mug sat across from her. There was a fresh pot of coffee on the stove along with pies, cakes, cookies, and snacks.

"Hey, Baby," she said.

"What's going on?" I asked.

The house smelled like a lemon cake. I searched around for it. I knew it was in there somewhere. "We're having Bible study in the basement. Everyone is going to be so happy to see you," Mama said. "Want to join us?"

"Sure," I told her. I hadn't been to Bible study in years.

I placed the Popeye's chicken down on the kitchen table along with my keys and purse, then I joined Alto-vise and Tita in the living room on the couch.

As soon I sat down, the cramps began again. When I stood up, water ran down my leg. I screamed.

Tita yelled, "Her water broke all over your floor, Mama Bond."

I held my stomach and said, "I'm in labor."

"Oh, Lord, I just cleaned my floors," Mama said as she ran into the living room.

I was terrified. I stood there like a deer caught in headlights. I was afraid that if I moved the baby would slide out. I know it sounds silly, but I was a new Mama. I didn't know.

Once my family realized I really was in labor and I had to be helped to the car, Mama and Altovise took my hand and walked me out the back door and down the back stairs. Tita was in the Range and had it running. I don't know how he got the keys or how he knew I was in the Range.

Mama told me to calm down and breathe. I did exactly as she said. Then, I had the sudden urge to push this turkey out of me.

"Mama," I cried, "I wanna push."

Mama said, "Don't push, Baby, we're almost at the hospital."

"Mama, look under her dress and see if you see the baby crowning," Altovise said.

Mama frowned and told her, "I think it's too early for that."

But she pulled down my wet panties anyway as she said to me, "I'm sorry, Baby, for violating you."

Mama looked under my dress.

After about a minute, Altovise yelled, "Mama, what the hell is taking you so long?"

Mama looked up and said, "We about to have a baby."

Altovise screamed. Tita screamed. I screamed.

Mama yelled, "Calm down, calm down. We have to do this."

She was out of breath and sweat poured from her face.

"Ashanti," she said, "You are so brave to have this baby in the back of your Range Rover."

"I'm not having my baby in the back of this car!" I yelled. "Drive, dammit, drive!"

Chapter Twenty-Three

WELCOME TO MY HOLIDAY, LOVE

We were slammed. We ran out of just about everything. Before I left for the day, I put in a small order. I made some adjustments to the inventory that arrived at 4:00 p.m. instead of 5:00 p.m. I knew my staff would fuss but I'd rather they fuss than to be out of something and miss out on cash.

I made desserts for the sweethearts booth and the bakery. I melted chocolate for the fondue display at the front of the restaurant. It can get messy at times, but customers enjoy it. My eyes were burning and I had not eaten a thing since 12:00 p.m.

Lyell, my father's jump off or whatever you want to call her this week, and my dad came down for lunch for her birthday. We sat outside on the patio. I made crab cakes, salmon, lobster tails, melted some butter, and put a few steaks on. Pop loves my salmon with butter and wild rice.

It was just the three of us on the patio chatting and watching the sailboats come in. Pop kept checking his phone and leaving. I told myself that when I had some free time, I was going to check him on it. I thought he was being rude, but being the man that I am, I kept quiet.

Well, check this out. When Pop left for the third time, Lyell eased over to me, put her hand on my dick, and rubbed it through my pants. I didn't stop her. I let her have her way. I wanted to take her into the bathroom and suck on her tits, but she belonged to my pop. But Pop was not interested in her. He was probably digging out some other nasty chick or her friend. I laughed Lyell's advance off and told her that I loved Ashanti.

Lyell smiled as she wrapped those red lips around her glass and sipped.

I thought to myself, *She's older. She knows how to suck a dick. Look at those dick sucking lips.*

Monica surprised Lyell with a strawberry shortcake for dessert. Thank goodness. I had to think about all types of crazy shit to keep my dick down. She was coming for it and I was going to give it to her. I'm weak.

After all that good eating, I needed a nap. I went into my office, closed the door, and turned the air up just a little bit since everybody was complaining about how hot it was. I kicked back in my swivel chair and closed my eyes. Then, somebody knocked on the door.

Monica yelled through the door, "Jaime, the O's game just let out and people are piling in."

We were slammed from 4:00 p.m. until 9:00 p.m. The bar was packed. We were on an hour wait. Most of the people hung out on the patio, sipped beer, smoked at the high tops, and ate wings and jalapeño poppers. Monica ran the patio. She is the best.

Since my mother and Pete have been gone, I've been keeping busy. I haven't had a chance to go through my mother's personal items at her condo yet. I had planned to go in the morning, but something told me to go that night.

It was the day before our baby shower; the perfect time to go over to my mother's and begin clearing things out. I'd decided to sell her belongings because I didn't need them. I left without letting Ashanti know where I was going. I made sure I had the key to Mama's condo. When I arrived, the young lady at the front desk handed me a pile of mail. I thanked her and headed up to Mama's place.

I turned on the light and looked around the luxurious condo. After all this time, I could still smell her. I walked into the living room. There was a box on the floor. I knelt down and looked inside. It was a box full of the pictures that had been on the wall. Tears welled up in my eyes and slid down my face before I had a chance to catch them. Mama had a picture of Ashanti and I on our wedding day.

There was also a recent picture of Ashanti and I in front of our faux fireplace. We took that picture about two months before Mama died. I don't know how she got it, but she had it.

She had a lot of pictures of Ashanti. That made me tear up even more. I never knew Mama took anything from the wedding. She acted as if that was the worst day of her life. But, judging by all of the pictures and programs she kept, she felt something. That made me smile. I was starting to feel better.

I went into her bedroom and searched through her drawers. I felt bad. It felt like I was violating her space. I came across an envelope that read: "Ashanti and Baby." It was heavy. Money was in it. I didn't count it, I just put it in my back pocket.

There was an envelope for me in her drawer as well, but it was flat. I sat on the edge of the bed and opened it. It was a check for a million dollars.

Damn, Mama. On top of all that you already left me, you left me this too, I thought.

I knew I had to do something smart with the money, as soon as my heart stopped racing.

There was an envelope for Rachael too.

Oh, hell no. I know she not giving this chick anything.

I opened the envelope. It was a letter that read:

Rachael,

I know that your daughter is not my son's. I can look her in the eyes and tell that she is not a Harris. The only reason I helped you was because you asked me to. I regret it. I regret you. I regret ever believing in you over my daughter-in-law and most importantly my son. It put a hole in my heart that was never filled. And now that I am dying, it is too late to say to my beautiful daughter-in-law that I am sorry.

I caused her pain for far too long and going against her to side with you was like going against my only son, Jaime. So, when I am dead and gone, I want you gone. Disappear out of his life like you did when you found out you were pregnant.

Clairess

Wow!

I put the envelope in my pocket and made a mental note to give it to Rachael. I didn't know how to go about getting it to her, but she'd get it.

I went home to Ashanti. She'd made spaghetti and meatballs, salad, and garlic bread. She also had store-bought chocolate cake. She didn't tell me that she was having a family dinner though. By the time I got there, the family was having the chocolate cake with coffee.

"Hello, Everyone."

I tried my best not to let anyone know that I'd cried on the way over, but Ashanti could tell. She stood up from the couch and smiled. We made our way to the kitchen and I handed her the envelope.

"It's from Mama."

She took the envelope, looked inside, and gasped.

"I know," I said. "I did the same thing."

"Are you for real?" she asked.

"What are you going to do with the money?"

She said, "Pay some bills. Get ready for the baby."

There was a long pause between us. Then, she bit her bottom lip, closed her eyes, and handed the envelope back to me.

"Here, take it."

I was confused, but I took the envelope and placed it in my back pocket again.

"I trust you."

"Ashanti, Baby. What if I told you that I would like to open another restaurant? I want to be like the dude that made Friday's. Open a Pete's in Vegas or Florida or Texas. Let's take this global. Leave the kids something to look forward to."

"Kids? Plural?" Ashanti asked then laughed. "I have to do this again?"

We both laughed.

"Baby," she said. "I believe in you. Do what makes you happy."

She walked closer to me, stood on the tips of her toes, kissed my lips and said, "I love you."

Elliott interrupted, "Hey, I'm going to call it a night. Thank you."

"No problem. What's wrong?" Ashanti asked.

"I am not feeling well."

"Oh no," Ashanti gasped.

I laughed. I told her she couldn't cook.

"Was it my spaghetti?" she asked Elliott.

She looked terrified, but I couldn't help myself. The shit was funny. I lowered my head in my chest and laughed harder.

Then, I broke the awkward silence and said, "I hope you feel better, Elliott. Have a good night."

"I'll walk you out," Ashanti said as she walked her brother to his car.

♥

Ashanti kept me up all night. I wanted to stay close to her because the baby was due any day. He didn't want to come out though. I wanted to stay with my wife, but I had to go to work.

I was barely at the restaurant due to traveling and being on television. Plus, I had been approached to write a cookbook. My life was hectic. Ever since Mama passed, I hadn't stopped. I'm like Diddy, I can't stop. I want more for my people, my community. I want to go global and help young black men like myself. I want to let them know they can be just as great as me.

I want to tell them, "Don't let your skin color define you, you are just as good as the next man. I know I had the upper hand with money, but the cats I know work hard. They drive better cars than I do and they doing just as well as me with the women. I'm ready to take over the world.

I called Ashanti to see what she was up to. She said she was on her way out the door to get some Popeyes and head over to her mother's. I think she wanted the Popeyes and was making excuses to get it. She knows I am not a fan of Popeyes. I cannot stand their chicken.

Anyway, when I got to work, I had a pre-shift meeting with the staff. I asked everyone to put in bids for vacations and had to remind them that they cannot all leave at once. I also had to remind them that I needed them since I would be out for a couple weeks with Ashanti and the baby, along with opening the other restaurant. We went over who wanted to help and I told them that if they knew anybody that needed a job to tell them to apply in person. I'm old school. I like having paper applications and I want to see you before I call you in for an interview.

I seasoned and rubbed a rack of ribs and was about to put them in the oven when Ashanti's aunt, Belle, rushed into the kitchen.

"Jaime, Altovise is on the phone. Ashanti went into labor."

As I turned towards Belle, I dropped the ribs on the floor. She laughed. I was frazzled.

"Where is she?" I asked. "Is she at the hospital?"

"Come on, Suga."

Belle took my hand. I was shaking like a leaf.

"I have to get my camera, my iPad, and my phone," I said. "And, I need my keys. I need my keys to my car. Where is my car?"

"In the garage where you left it this morning," Belle said calmly as I went into the office to grab everything I needed.

Well, Belle grabbed all the things I needed. I was trying to get in contact with Ashanti, but no one was answering her phone.

When we arrived at the hospital, I was told that Ashanti was pushing. I was handed a pair of scrubs and hurriedly put them on as I rushed into Ashanti's room.

Ashanti looked up with tears in her eyes and said, "Baby."

I walked over to her.

"Why are you crying?" I asked as I kissed her forehead, rubbed her face, and told her to calm down.

The doctor told Ashanti to push, so she balanced her weight on her elbows and belted out a mean ass growl. I looked down there. The baby's head was crowing. I was not feeling good. I had to get it together. I had to be there for my wife. I was dizzy. I ain't never seen no shit like that before in my life.

Altovise was on the opposite side of the hospital bed wiping Ashanti's forehead. The doctor coached Ashanti. She sat up, balanced her weight on her elbows, pushed her head down in her chest, and before I knew it, the baby's head popped out.

Oh boy. I felt lightheaded. One more push and he will finally be here. Ashanti grabbed her knees, pushed down, and let out a piercing cry. He was coming. Next thing I knew, my wife reached between her legs and pulled him out. Altovise cracked up. I stood there with my mouth wide open. Did she really pull his ass from her pussy like that? Could she do that?

I guess she could. I kissed her on the forehead. She was trying to catch her breath. She looked over at me and smiled. Our son was covered in blood.

As he laid on Ashanti's chest, he didn't make a sound. His eyes were wide and brown like his mother's. She looked down at him. He was our greatest accomplishment together.

"Happy birthday, Jaime," she whispered into his ear.

They took him, weighed him, and cleaned him up. Jaime Harris III was born on June 12. He weighed nine pounds, seven ounces, and he was nineteen inches long. He was beautiful.

Ashanti looked over at Altovise and said, "That shit hurt."

"You did it though. And you made it look so easy," Altovise said as she wiped tears from her eyes.

Chapter Twenty-Four

LOVES HOLIDAY

There is my baby. My baby love. Baby Jaime was kicking and laughing. He had just turned three months. He was the fattest, happiest baby. This little boy is the best thing that ever happened to Jaime and me. We took turns feeding and changing and staying up with him. I only went into the restaurant a few hours a week to help out. Nothing major. Elliott and Sherri were running the real estate business. They were doing a wonderful job. Sherri got her real estate license. Elliott was doing all of the secretarial work. I was appreciative. I went in from time to time to check on them. When I did, I took the baby with me. We went to seminars and classes together. I did whatever it took to keep them educated and well informed.

Most new parents need a break, but nobody gets my baby. My mother even asked if Jaime and I wanted some time alone, but we were okay. I do not let my baby out of my sight. Jaime and I would make love after the baby fell asleep at night. We had romantic dinners. We even walked around the house naked. The baby don't know what's going on. Most of the time he was naked too.

"Hey, Baby," I said as Jaime walked in.

I was in the baby's room changing him. He was fighting a losing battle against sleep.

"Hey," Jaime responded.

"Betty Morgan called," I said as I rocked the baby to sleep.

Surprised, Jaime asked, "She called you?"

Was Betty not supposed to call me? He was acting weird.

"Yeah," I laughed as I folded Jaime III's clothes.

"She called my phone this morning and asked if she could interview us for the *Baltimore* magazine."

The baby was a bit fussy. I closed his drawer, grabbed him from the crib, and placed his binky in his mouth. When he calmed down, I put him back into the crib.

"And you said?" Jaime asked.

Jaime was really getting on my nerves. I mean, come on, are you and Betty doing something illegal? I held my tongue. I know he's been under a lot of stress but I didn't need him coming up in here playing detective cause a little old white lady called me.

"I told her, 'Jaime will call you when he gets home.' What's the problem?"

"She just wants to be nosy."

Here we go. I am so sick of this shit.

He continued, "My father had an affair with her back in the day. Rumor is she has a son that looks just like me. I don't want no part of her."

"Wow. Who didn't your father sleep with?"

Jaime shrugged. Something was bothering him. I walked out of the baby's room and went into the kitchen.

He followed. There was a knock at the door. Jaime sat down at the kitchen counter.

I rushed to open it and saw Mama standing there.

"Mama…"

"I got set out."

She had all of her things in plastic bags; at least six bags worth. She placed them down by the door, walked into the kitchen, washed her hands, and said to Jaime, "Something smells good."

"Ma, what do you mean?" I asked.

"Where is the baby?"

"I just put him down for his nap. What happened?"

"Your father's gambling. I lost everything, even the business."

"Ma…"

"I am closing on Monday."

I couldn't believe my ears. There was another knock on the door. I told my mother to stay put. I had to get to the bottom of this. I opened the door. Daddy rushed into the house.

"I thought I'd find you here!" he yelled.

"Excuse me but my child is sleeping," I exhaled. "Excuse me…"

Jaime gave me that look. I paused. He was not happy. I followed him into the bedroom.

"What?" I asked.

"They got set out?"

"Yes."

He was pissed. I've never seen a man his complexion turn that red.

"I thought they owned the house?" Jaime asked.

I was dumbfounded. Jaime rubbed his forehead.

He said, "They can't stay here. Sorry."

I could not believe what I was hearing.

"Are you fucking kidding me? You selfish son of a bitch. Jaime, they are my parents," I responded.

Jaime shrugged. I couldn't believe he did not want my parents here in their time of need.

"Ashanti, I am tired."

"They are my mother and father."

I wanted to rip his fucking head off.

"Why do we have to step in and help? I am trying to raise my son."

"Jaime, please."

"I'm out. I'm done," he said as he pulled two duffle bags from the closet and filled them up with clothes. "Your parents... I know. When my father left my mother, he did not come running."

He zipped his bags and continued, "I am going to my father's. I am under a lot of stress. Call me in the morning. I love you."

And with that, he left. My head was spinning. I'd talk to him in the morning. Right now, I had to deal with my parents.

Chapter Twenty-Five

YESTERDAY

Ashanti and I are falling apart at the seams. She doesn't seem to understand that I want to try to live a normal life. Every time I look up, here comes her family or a friend and their kids with their hand out looking for something. I was sick of it. I lost my mother. I lost Pete. I am a new father opening businesses and gaining notoriety from my peers in the cooking industry. I don't need unnecessary stress.

I unpacked as soon as I got to my father's. I had to be at the restaurant at 6:00 a.m., so I set my Bulgari watch for 4:30 a.m. then placed it on the nightstand. I laid in the bed in my boxers and shirt looking at the ceiling.

There was a knock at the door. I looked out the peep hole. I couldn't see. I opened the door. She burst in with a bottle of Dom.

"Hey. You're James' son?"

"Jaime."

"Nice to meet you. He's supposed to meet me here."

She is beautiful. Who is this woman? I thought to myself.

"You are?" I asked her.

"Blaise," she said as she extended her hand.

She looked exactly like her name––beautiful, tall, shapely, and sexy with a head full of real hair. She was sexy as hell. Did I mention she was sexy? Where was Lyell? My father is a player. Blaise must have been who took up my father's attention at the restaurant on Lyell's birthday. I see why. Lyell is sexy as fuck, but Blaise got it going on. Damn. She has the longest dancer legs. She looks around Pop's age, maybe fifty-nine or sixty. She is a sophisticated, mature, grown, sexy woman, and she smelled good too, like coconut and vanilla. Her skin is a beautiful shade of chocolate. Her melanin is popping. Jesus. I've never seen a more perfect human being before in my life.

"Would you like some bubbly?" she asked me.

"No thanks."

My stomach was growling.

"Hungry?" I asked her.

"Yes."

"I'll whip us up something."

I went into the bedroom, put on my jeans and a shirt, then returned to the kitchen. Pop had some steaks in the fridge marinating. Blaise popped open the bottle. By the time I got the vegetables diced and the potatoes on the grill, the bottle was almost gone. Damn. I listened as Blaise talked about her family and how much she loved my father.

I placed three potatoes, vegetables, and the sizzling steaks straight from the grill onto a ceramic plate. We were about to eat when Pop walked in.

"Hey, Baby," Blaise greeted him.

"Hey, you trying to take my woman?" Pop asked as he kissed Blaise.

"Jaime made a wonderful steak," Blaise said as she winked at me.

"You were supposed to cook, Blaise," Pop said as he sat with us at the table.

Blaise shrugged her shoulders. She was on her second bottle of champagne.

"I couldn't get into the kitchen," she said jokingly.

"Ashanti and I had a fight," I said to Pop.

Blaise stood, "He can stay."

Pop frowned and his forehead wrinkled as he said, "No he can't."

Then he snickered and asked, "Where is my plate?"

"Baby, we can sleep in the guest room."

"How am I a guest in my own condo? I got this place so no one would come here," Pop said.

He can act like a baby sometimes. I just laughed at him.

"Jaime," Blaise returned to the table with another bottle of wine. "Dessert?"

"I can whip up some pudding."

"Do that," Pop said.

♥

The next morning, Pop and I were up at 4:00 a.m. working out. Blaise was knocked out on the couch. I asked Pop if she had come to bed.

He said, "Nope, and I wasn't looking for her."

"What happened to Lyell?"

"She's still around. She was pressing the marriage issue. Waited until your mama was dead and gone then started acting up. We needed a break."

"I thought you loved her?" I asked him.

He responded, "I thought you loved Ashanti."

"She does not get it."

"Talk to her then. Are you happy?"

"I am in love. I just need space."

"Get an apartment or a condo."

"Had one. Got rid of it."

"Why don't you go stay at your mother's old place?"

Pop tossed a bottle of water across the room. I caught it.

"She never used it. The bitch had like nine houses," he continued.

We laughed.

"There is a rental on the third floor, I can put in a good word for you. You need it."

I didn't tell Ashanti about the place. Once Pop put in the good word for me, it was mine. I invited the property manager down to the restaurant to have dinner with me. She said it was cool but only if she could bring her two kids. I love the kids, so I told her sure. I had to let her know I was appreciative of what she had done for me and I wasn't looking for nothing from her. I moved in the next day.

I got a dining room and a bedroom set for myself along with baby furniture for my boy. Of course, I set the kitchen up nice. I don't plan on leaving my wife, I just need some time to gather my thoughts. I haven't really mourned and I feel empty inside. It's like I'm going out of my damn mind. Losing a loved one hurts but losing a parent hurts worse. I kept expecting my mother to walk through the door saying, "No more leather" or telling me how to put this or that up. I called Ashanti. She was concerned about my whereabouts. I told her I was okay and not to worry about me. She asked me to come home. I asked her to respect my wishes not to. She said okay, but I knew she wasn't alright with my decision.

I invited Red and the kitchen crew over to my new place. I asked them not to mention anything about it to Ashanti or anyone at the restaurant.

Red examined the place like I was going to let him have a room.

"Man, this place is nice as shit."

Cecil, Cecil's son, Damien, and Brian also showed up. Cecil bought some wings. Red had the weed. Damien is a damn slug. I told Cecil to keep his ass away from me. I don't have anything against him, but he is a fucking creep.

"Nice view man," Brian said to me and nodded. "This is my first time hanging out with you outside of work. You cool as shit." He sipped some beer. "When my mom called me, she kept talking about this steak you made."

Brian began working at the restaurant about a week or so ago. I don't know him like that but a lot of dudes in the kitchen said he was cool.

"Blaise your mama?" I asked.

We were at the bar sipping Heinekens. Red was on the other side of the bar rolling a blunt. I don't trust him with the marijuana. He likes to lace it with shit.

"Yeah," Brian said as he tipped the beer in my direction.

I nodded.

"She's dating your father."

"Yeah, I was over there three nights last week cooking dinner. She is a nice woman."

"She wants to marry your pops."

"Pops been through a lot. I am sure if they love each other the way they say they do, and I see it, they will."

"My man."

"Excuse me…"

♥

I excused myself, went into my bedroom, closed my door, and sat on the edge of the bed. Then, I reached for the phone.

"Jaime, man is the wings done?" Red asked from outside my bedroom door.

This nigga cooks buffalo wings better than I do and has the nerve to ask me were they done?

"Yeah man," I said as tears rolled down my face. "Take them out."

I prayed that no one came in and saw me crying. It was after 11:00 p.m. I figured she was asleep, but I took a chance and called.

"Hello."

I cleared my throat.

"Hey. How are you?"

"Hey, Jaime, I'm fine. What's wrong?"

I asked her about the baby. She said they had gone to the zoo and to the park and now he was sleeping right beside her. I asked did he have a good time. She said he loved the monkeys. I asked could I come and see her. Silence. I know she did not want to see me.

Then, she broke her silence and said, "Sure. See you in a few."

Chapter Twenty-Six

LOVE'S IN NEED OF A HOLIDAY

I was seething when he called. I had not seen my husband since the birth of my child; he was almost six months old now. Jaime had lost it. He made it hard for the family. My mother and I shared the condo. She helped out with the baby. I don't know where I would be without her. She cooked, cleaned, and did the laundry while I worked. My husband was wherever the hell he wanted to be. I had to go back to work as soon as my six weeks was up. I didn't want to. I had to. I was also in the process of getting my mother her house back. I could not sit idly by and allow the house to go on the market. We grew up in that house. Besides, I love my mother, but she could not live with me forever.

It was a week before Thanksgiving. It took me six months to get Mama the house back. I paid off all the debts she owed, and we even opened another bakery. My father was not allowed anywhere near anything. I refused to have him come around and destroy what I had rebuilt. I told him to go back to the woman that he was spending Mama's money on. Yeah. He cheated. He wasn't good at it. He was very sloppy. It was like he wanted to get caught. I asked Mama what she wanted to do. She said she wanted to work on the marriage.

I said, "Ok. Have fun. You, him, her, and the baby."

Yeah, the girl was six months pregnant when I found out about her. Altovise said she had no clue Daddy was fucking someone else. No one did. But when we found out, it was awful.

Mama went to therapy. She was a mess. It was quite the scandal. And you know what happens when news spreads in a church. Fix it Jesus.

Jaime came over that night. He was remorseful. I almost felt sorry for him. He had slept around on me. On my life, I wanted to kill him when I found out I had a STD after our son was born. Can you imagine? I was sick for weeks. I didn't want any parts of him. You make all this money, but you can't wrap it up? What the fuck? I was done.

♥

We were having our holiday meeting, going over the budgets and schedules. Jaime's phone rang. He got up and left without saying a word. The nerve of him to leave during the most important meeting of the year to probably go see a woman. Van, Mila, and I sat waiting for almost twenty minutes until I decided to call him. His phone went to voicemail. Okay. I finished the meeting. It wasn't fair for us to wait on him while he was out doing only God knows what.

Once the meeting was over, Van and Mila headed back to work. I sat and waited for Jaime to return to the office for as long as I could but it was getting late, I was tired, and I had to get home.

I was coming out of the office when I bumped into him.

"What's up?" I asked as we went back into the office.

"How'd it go?" he asked while fixing his pants.

I shook my head in disgust and walked away from him.

"You couldn't wait?" I asked.

Jaime lowered his head as I turned towards him.

"Can you at least do it behind my back or make it seem like you're happy?" I asked. "At work Jaime?"

"I want to leave."

I inhaled slowly then exhaled even slower. I was hurt. Betrayed. But you know what? It felt better than looking like a fool.

"Who is she?"

"There is no one else."

"You haven't made it official yet?" I asked. "But you leave work for an hour, come back with nut stains on your pants, and you expect everything to be good? Come in here and just want me to accept you leaving me and your child?"

"I want us to work together, raise our son together, and pretend."

"I'm not your mother, Jaime." I shook my head no as I backed away from him. "I'm not putting up no damn façade. You want to leave? Leave. I cannot make no grown man stay where he don't want to be. If she means that much to you, leave."

Jaime charged towards me and said, "It's not like that. God, Ashanti!"

He exhaled.

"I just need some time to think."

"You can have all the time you need. Don't think you can come back whenever you want and expect for me to pick up where we left off like you never left. You leave, you stay gone."

"I will take care of you and Jaime."

"You damn right you will. I want a divorce," I cried. "I can't do this. You are impossible. You are not the man I fell in love with."

He took my hands in his.

"Ashanti."

I snatched my hands back.

"I haven't been happy for a while," I said. "The only thing that brings me joy is my child. I can't go on pretending that I am happy with you when I am not. I am disappointed in you. You let me down. You let our family down. I can't."

Jaime held his head in his hands.

"Not now, Ashanti," he said.

"Goodbye, Jaime."

And just like that, I walked away.

♥

That takes us back to chapter one. He said he needed his space; he wanted to leave. I had to let him know how I felt. It was hard.

I'm hurt. Words cannot describe the pain I am feeling. I don't remember the last time I fell asleep with a dry pillow or woke up without a knot in my throat. The sun never shines as bright as it used to and the rain hurts as it hits my skin when I run through the raindrops. Holidays are not as jolly. Santa doesn't exist. The Easter Bunny made his eggs harder to find. All the hearts are broken on Valentine's Day. The turkey is dry on Thanksgiving and the floats on the parade route are deflated. Snow is not pure and white. The Fourth of July fireworks aren't as bright. Labor Day is filled with labor pains. Memorial Day is just a memorial. New Year's is just another day.

People are in your life for a reason, a season, or a lifetime. I don't know what is going to happen between Jaime and me. I am so hurt and confused. I don't know how I'm going to make it through this little life of mine. I'm in need of another holiday. Can I get a do over?

ABOUT THE AUTHOR

Monica Lynn is a writer and licensed cosmetologist with twenty years' experience. Focused on her mission to inspire and entertain, she has authored several novels and is currently working on the sequel to *Loves Holiday*.

Monica received her cosmetology license from Baltimore Studio of Hair Design School of Cosmetology. Her hobbies are singing, reading, baking, traveling, and she has a passion for fashion. Monica currently resides in Baltimore, Maryland.

Learn more at www.dreamtheglamgoddess.com